Ten
POWER PRINCIPLES
for
CHRISTIAN SERVICE

Other Titles by Warren W. Wiersbe (Selected)

Being a Child of God
Be Myself (autobiography)
The Bible Exposition Commentary (2 vols.)
The Bumps Are What You Climb On
Developing a Christian Imagination
Elements of Preaching
God Isn't in a Hurry: Learning to Slow Down and Live
The Integrity Crisis
On Being a Servant of God
Prayer, Praise, and Promises: A Daily Walk through the Psalms
So That's What a Christian Is! 12 Pictures of the Dynamic Christian Life
Turning Mountains into Molehills: And Other Devotional Talks
Victorious Christians You Should Know
Wiersbe's Expository Outlines on the New Testament
Wiersbe's Expository Outlines on the Old Testament

Ten POWER PRINCIPLES for CHRISTIAN SERVICE

Ministry Dynamics for a New Century

Warren W. & David W. WIERSBE

Baker Books

A Division of Baker Book House Co
Grand Rapids, Michigan 49516

© 1997 by Warren W. Wiersbe and David W. Wiersbe

Published by Baker Books
a division of Baker Publishing Group
P.O. Box 6287, Grand Rapids, MI 49516–6287
www.bakerbooks.com

Eighth printing, June 2006

Printed in the United States of America

Library of Congress Cataloging-in-Publication Date
Wiersbe, Warren W.
    Ten power principles for Christian service : ministry dynamics for a new century / Warren W. & David W. Wiersbe.
       p. cm.
    Includes bibliographical references and indexes.
    ISBN 10: 0-8010-9029-6 (pbk.)
    ISBN 978-0-8010-9029-5 (pbk.)
    1. Pastoral theology. 2. Clergy—Office. I. Wiersbe, David. II. Title.
BV4011.W47 1997
253—dc21   97–6648

Contents

Preface

*I*n 1983, we published a book for ministerial students called *Making Sense of the Ministry.* Its success was modest, and in 1989, Baker Book House issued a second, enlarged edition. The response from seminary personnel, pastors, and students was encouraging, but we discovered that chapters 3 and 4 ("Some Principles of Ministry") were considered by many to be the best part of the book.

When Chuck Swindoll read these ten principles over his "Insight for Living" radio program it created new interest in the book, but by then it was out of print and not scheduled for reprinting. Our friend and editor, Jim Weaver, at Baker Book House suggested a book expanding on each of the ten principles designed for both ministers and ministerial students.

Since we represent two different "ministerial generations," we tried to achieve some sort of balance in an age when churches seem to be going from one extreme to another. We hope we succeeded. This is not a time for "generation bashing."

Both of us are busy in ministry, so it wasn't easy to find time to share ideas, write, and assess our work. But thanks to telephones, computers, machines, and the blessing of the Lord, and a lot of patience on the part of our publisher, we have completed the book.

We trust that what we've written will not only help God's seasoned servants as they minister in an age of change, but will also encourage ministerial students and younger pastors as they get started in their work. In spite of the bad press the church occasionally receives, there are some great things happening among God's people, especially pastors, and we rejoice in it. If we build on principles, our work will endure. If we embrace every new idea that comes along, without reflection, we will find ourselves only trying to hug the wind.

The stories about pastors and churches used in these chapters are fictional. If you think we've written about you, your church, or somebody you know in ministry, please be sure that you're mistaken. Unfortunately, the bad situations we describe frequently occur in churches because people are people, and the good situations we write about don't occur enough.

Over the years, we have both been helped by reading books about ministry, so if this book brings encouragement to other ministers, we are grateful. This is one way to repay the great debt that we owe to others.

Warren W. Wiersbe
David W. Wiersbe

Introduction

The Tale
of Two Churches

"T his will probably be our last pastorate," John Chandler said to his wife as they unpacked the everyday dishes and put them the dishwasher. "But I think it will be our best."

"I agree with you," Martha replied encouragingly, as she always did. To her, John Chandler was the greatest preacher who ever lived, and the thirty-two years they'd served together had been exciting and enriching.

John went on. "The Lord willing, I'm good for the next six or seven years. And then it's off to that little house in Colorado, where I'll have lots of time for reading and fishing and doing whatever pulpit ministry the Lord opens up for me."

"Well, you certainly have plenty of experience to draw on from our last three churches," Martha said. "Your ideas have always worked and they'll work here at Briarwood. This is our first suburban church, so let's enjoy it. They wouldn't have called you if they didn't think you could do the job."

But Pastor Chandler didn't do the job. After eight painful months as pastor of Briarwood New Life Fellowship, he was ready to quit. In spite of his excellent track record in previous pastorates, almost every idea John had suggested at Briarwood had been turned down by the members of his young suburban congregation.

At first John was baffled by this response and walked away from board meetings muttering, "Baby boomers!" Then he became bitter and hardly spoke to the church officers at all. Finally, feeling that his time was short, he became belligerent and unfortunately started to make enemies in the church. That was when Tom Harris, chairman of the board, stepped in to rescue him.

"Pastor, the church loves you and wants you to stay and the board wants you to stay. Youngsters like us need leaders like you and Martha. You've got the kind of maturity and experience that have enriched all of us. It's just that you're going to have to accept us as we are and learn to go with the flow."

"But nobody's accepted one idea I've presented!" John protested. "I feel like a reject."

"Then stop presenting ideas for a few months. Just live with us, preach to us the way you did when you first came, get to know us, and then together we'll work out the future. You have some growing to do and so do we. I admit we're younger and different, and you'll have some adjusting to do; but together we can make this ministry work."

John thanked Tom; he talked the matter over with Martha, and they prayed together. They agreed to stay, come what may. John started meeting the young leaders personally and Martha visited with their wives, and before long all of them bonded. Today John laughs at the dumb things he did "trying to make people grow up overnight," and he confesses his bad attitude toward "that younger generation." Today, Briarwood New Life Fellowship is exploding with power and people, and John is grooming his associate to become the next senior pastor.

Kevin and Karen Randall were excited as they read the letter from Grace Bible Church. They had been accepted! After four years of Bible college and three years of graduate work, Kevin was at last going to serve the Lord in his first pastorate with his bride of three years at his side to help him.

"The potential at Grace Church really challenges me," Kevin said as he packed his precious seminary notebooks. Pointing to the box, he said, "Why, there are enough ministry ideas in those notebooks to keep that church on the move for years to come. I can hardly wait to put all those great programs to work."

"And little Kandy will enjoy growing up in a quiet small town like Greenfield," said Karen. "She'll have so many adopted grandmothers and grandfathers, she'll probably become spoiled!"

But Kandy almost didn't get the opportunity to be spoiled in Greenfield. Exactly one year later, Kevin was ready to write his resignation and Karen was starting to pack, this time without enthusiasm and joy. However, when Kevin gave his resignation to the board, effective immediately, they wouldn't accept it.

"Son," George Saunders said quietly. "You don't want to quit. I know we're not an easy bunch to shepherd; but if you'll stay with us, we'll all learn together and get the job done."

"But nobody seems to want to follow me," Kevin protested. "You all treat me like your son or grandson instead of like your pastor."

"Well," said George smiling, "didn't Paul tell Timothy to treat the older men like fathers?" He opened the big Bible he always carried to church and read 1 Timothy 5:1: "Do not rebuke an older man, but exhort him as a father" (NKJV).

Kevin was silent. Then Harry Preston spoke up. "Pastor Kevin, we love you and Karen and we want you to stay and work with us. This old church needs to open the windows and let in some fresh air, and we think you can do it. But old sheep like us can't be driven; we have to be led patiently. You've got some new ideas that sort of scare some of us; but if you'll give us time, we'll catch up."

Kevin picked up his resignation and put it in his pocket.

"I guess I owe you men an apology. I wanted *you* to be teachable, but I wasn't very teachable myself. We all want to see the church alive and growing. It's just that we look at it from two different perspectives."

The prayer meeting that followed indicated that what could have been a Waterloo turned out to be a watershed. They had turned the corner.

What went wrong in the ministries of these four dedicated servants of God? The Chandlers and the Randalls were devoted to the Lord and eager to serve. They were called by congregations who must have felt that they were doing God's will when they invited them to come to their churches and serve. Yet after John and Kevin had said "I do" to these churches, neither man hardly had time for a joyful honeymoon, let alone a happy marriage. There were almost two "church divorces," painful to both the pastors and the congregations.

While it's possible that the Chandlers were mismatched to their suburban "baby boomer" church, that wasn't the major problem. John's basic failure was his seeming inability to adapt his past successes to his present challenges. He'd received his training during the forties and fifties, when the "classical period" of ministerial education was cresting in America; but by the time he arrived at his final pastorate, things had radically changed in American society and in local churches.

The principles on which John had based his successful ministry in three previous churches worked in the fourth congregation after he learned to understand the people he was ministering to. Once John started stretching himself, instead of imitating himself, he felt the challenge of the young congregation and began to minister effectively. "I feel ten years younger pastoring this crowd!" he told Martha, and he looked it.

As for the Randalls, it would be easy to say that they lacked experience and were idealistic and naive; perhaps some of this was true. But when they dropped into traditional Grace Bible Church in the graying town of Greenfield, they became "baby *bomb*ers" instead of "baby boomers," and the explosion almost cost them dearly. While Pastor John Chandler had initially failed to adapt the old to the new, Kevin and Karen weren't too skilled at applying the new to the old. The "establishment mentality" of Grace Church's leaders automatically resisted the young couple's ideas and lifestyle. Unwilling to spend his formative pastoral years cosmetizing a corpse, Kevin decided to resign. If he had left, Kevin and Karen both would have missed a great learning experience among people who really loved them.

It's unfortunate that these two pastors and their congregations experienced so much grief. Once the pastors accepted their people, loved them, and learned from them, and the churches patiently prayed and determined to work with their shepherds, they all enjoyed a time of exciting personal growth that resulted in progress for both churches. At Briarwood, John felt like a patriarch in a day nursery; at Greenfield, Kevin felt like an obstetrician in a cemetery. When their expectations for their churches were not fulfilled, both men became discouraged, then demanding, and finally defiant. God had set before them an open door, but unfortunately they tried to hang an "exit" sign over it. God changed the sign to "opportunity."

We've written this book to help pastoral couples like the Chandlers and the Randalls, and churches like New Life Fellowship and Grace Bible Church. The answer to their problems wasn't to destroy the old and embrace the new, or embalm the old and resist the new. *The answer was to rediscover the basic principles of ministry that apply to all churches and ministries at all times, and to grow together while applying these principles.*

This book is about the unchanging principles of ministry, and our thesis is that obeying these principles leads to success in ministry. These principles aren't many, nor are they complicated. They haven't changed throughout history, although the methods of applying them have changed. A bit of anonymous verse says it well:

> Methods are many, principles are few;
> Methods always change, principles never do.

For example, it's a basic principle that Christian ministry must depend on the Word of God and prayer (Acts 6:4). *How* the pastor encourages his people to study the Word and pray will vary from church to church and place to place, and it's dangerous for the pastor to imitate what another church is doing just because "it works." *Methods* are the changing local applications of unchanging universal principles, and no method should be given the status that belongs only to a principle. When the methods we use are true to the principles of Scripture, our ministry will be successful. No matter how we or others may evaluate what we do, ministry that's based on biblical principles will meet human needs and glorify God. In his time, God will reward it.

The wise steward of God's serving grace (1 Peter 4:10) must exercise discernment both in understanding the biblical principles and in selecting the methods that best "flesh out" these principles in daily service. "Therefore every teacher of the law who has been instructed about the kingdom of heaven is like the owner of a house who brings out of his storeroom new treasures as well as old" (Matt. 13:52). In their feverish quest for change and novelty, some people ignore the old and forget that the new comes out of the old. They forget that both the new and the old are necessary for balance and progress in ministry. Embalm the old methods and you'll create an atmosphere in the church that will hinder the Spirit from doing anything new. But enthrone the new so that the old is neglected and you'll pull the roots right out of the ministry and eventually have a withering witness. Once John Chandler and Kevin Randall and their congregations realized that the old and the new are friends and not enemies, they enjoyed rewarding ministries in spite of the difficulties that always come with confrontation and change. Both the pastors and the churches grew because they faced facts honestly and followed God's principles humbly.

We're living at a time in history when the ages are colliding and God is shaking things in his church. But he's shaking things "so that the things which cannot be shaken may remain" (Heb.

12:27 NKJV). It's time for Christians to stop worrying about the scaffolding and start strengthening the foundations. We always need better methods for serving the Lord, but our methods must be tested by the principles laid down in Scripture.

It's not easy to evaluate ministry, and we all need to heed the admonition of Paul: "Therefore judge nothing before the appointed time; wait till the Lord comes. He will bring to light what is hidden in darkness and will expose the motives of men's hearts. At that time each will receive his praise from God" (1 Cor. 4:5). Only God knows which churches and ministries are successful, and one day he will tell us. Meanwhile, we must do our best to obey his Word and seek to please him.

"In matters of principle," said Thomas Jefferson, "stand like a rock; in matters of taste, swim with the current." The prophet Isaiah never met Jefferson, but he put those two images together— the rock and the river—when he wrote about leadership:

> Behold, a king will reign in righteousness, and princes will rule with justice. A man will be as a hiding place from the wind, and a cover from the tempest, as rivers of water in a dry place, as the shadow of a great rock in a weary land. (Isa. 32:1–2 NKJV)

As we seek to build the church, we need the strength and stability of the rock and the power and adaptability of the river. It's what philosopher Alfred North Whitehead described as "order in the midst of change and change in the midst of order." Principles are like rocks, and methods are like rivers; together they get the job done.

> The old is the womb out of which the new is born. Understand and appreciate the old and you'll see God give birth to the new and help you adapt it to your present situation.

Chapter One

The Foundation of Ministry Is Character

*P*astor Mike eased the car quietly into the driveway and turned off the ignition. He was hoping Dottie was asleep so he could slip into the house undetected, but she met him on the landing by their bedroom door.

"Long meeting," she commented.

"You know what church committee meetings are like," he replied with the masquerade of a smile. "You're up late yourself."

"I'm up late because we need to talk," she said.

"Let's talk tomorrow," Mike replied as he headed for the bedroom. "I'm beat."

"No, Mike. Now, right now. You'd better talk to *me* tonight before you talk to the police tomorrow."

Mike stopped and turned to face his wife, and for the first time he noticed that she'd been crying.

"The police?" he asked, trying to look surprised. "What would the police want with *me?*"

Dottie sat down on the edge of the bed and looked straight at her husband. It was a look that was both penetrating and painful.

"Mike, it's no use pretending. I know you weren't at a long meeting tonight. Sylvia phoned me when Art got home and she was surprised you weren't home yet. I know where you were. You were out cruising, and this time the police saw you and got the license number. They phoned me over an hour ago, and I begged them for the children's sake not to come out to the house." She paused, then said, "Mike, this time you're in trouble, deep trouble. We need to talk... *right now.*"

Helen was the first business manager of Faith Church, and she'd been on the job only four months when she began to get suspicious. In preparation for the annual stewardship campaign, she'd been reviewing the church financial records. She was convinced that somebody in the financial structure of the church was misappropriating funds.

The longer she prayed and pondered, the heavier the burden became, until she had to share it with Pastor Newman.

"That's a pretty serious accusation, Helen," said the pastor. "We've got to be careful or we'll create a scandal and maybe invite a lawsuit, and the church doesn't need either one. It isn't just money—it's the witness of the church that's at stake."

"What do we do?" Helen asked. "We can't let this go on."

"The first thing we do is get real evidence," Pastor Newman replied. "Let me chat with our banker. He's a fine Christian man and he can give us good counsel."

While the treasurer was out of town on a combined business trip and vacation, a private investigator got all the evidence the church needed. Their trusted treasurer had stolen over fifty thousand dollars from the church over a period of ten years. When he was confronted, he at first tried to bluster his way out of it; but the evidence was too substantial, and he finally broke down and confessed.

It was the same old story of secretly supporting expensive habits while away on business trips, another double life of sin that finally paid deadly wages.

In recent years, the media have been especially hard on people like Pastor Mike and the covetous church treasurer, people in ministry who live double lives and bring disgrace on themselves, their loved ones, and the gospel. Of course, we all know that ministry isn't the only place where hypocrites hide. Every profession has its hypocrites. Bankers steal money, athletes use drugs, lawyers fabricate evidence, politicians accept bribes, doctors peddle narcotics, and parents abuse their children. The church isn't the only "den of thieves" where culprits run to hide.[1] Human nature, being what it is, guarantees that we will find masqueraders in courtrooms, clinics, university lecture halls, federal offices, and even in homes that appear to be normal and happy.

But that's no excuse for "religious sin." The public expects more out of ministers of the gospel and the officers of the church, and rightly so, since Christian ministry is associated with *character*. After surveying the first seventy-five years of the "Lyman Beecher Lectures on Preaching," Batsell Barrett Baxter concluded, "There was no subject mentioned more often in the Lyman Beecher Lectures than that of the preacher's character." In the lectures, said Baxter, "the preacher's character was made the foundation upon which all else rises or falls."[2]

Phillips Brooks gave the Yale Lectures in 1876–77, and in them he defined preparation for ministry as "nothing less than the making of a man." He said:

> It cannot be the mere training to certain tricks. It cannot be even the furnishing with abundant knowledge. It must be nothing less than the kneading and tempering of a man's whole nature till it becomes of such a consistency and quality as to be capable of transmission.[3]

In one of his sermons, Brooks went so far as to define the "great purpose of life" as "the shaping of character by truth."[4] In other words, we may have talent, training, experience, reputation, and personality, but if we don't have character we don't have anything, for the foundation for ministry is character.

What Robert Murray M'Cheyne wrote to his missionary friend Daniel Edwards is as true today as it was in 1840:

> Remember you are God's sword—His instrument—I trust a chosen vessel unto Him to bear His name. In great measure, according to the purity and perfections of the instrument will be the success. It is not great talents God blesses so much as great likeness to Jesus. A holy minister is an awful weapon in the hand of God.[5]

Character is the raw material of life, out of which we either by diligence construct a temple or by negligence create a trash heap. Abraham Lincoln said that character was like a tree and reputation like the shadow of the tree. "The shadow is what we think of it," said Lincoln. "The tree is the real thing." Reputation is what people *think* we are; character is what God and the holy angels *know* we are. Evangelist D. L. Moody once said that character was "what a man is in the dark"; financial wizard J. P. Morgan called character the best collateral a person could give.

Character is what Jesus described in the Beatitudes and demonstrated in his own life and ministry in the Gospels. Character is made up of those beautiful qualities that Paul called the "fruit of the Spirit" in Galatians 5:22–23 and qualifications for office in 1 Timothy 3 and Titus 1. People with character have integrity; what they say and do comes from a heart fully dedicated to God.[6] Integrity means inner wholeness; we're not trying to fool others (hypocrisy) or fool ourselves (duplicity).

Character is Joseph saying "no" to Potiphar's wife and going to prison for being honest and chaste. It's Moses giving up the privileges of an Egyptian prince for the perils and problems of a Jewish prophet, and for forty years sacrificially serving a people who didn't deserve his leadership. It's Jeremiah devoting his lifetime to faithfully pleading with his people, and seeing the nation die before his very eyes. It's Paul saying, "Men and brethren, I have lived in all good conscience before God until this day" (Acts 23:1 NKJV), and getting slapped in the face for saying it. It's Martin Luther at the Diet of Worms declaring,

"Here stand I. I can do no other. God help me. Amen." It's Hugh Lattimer saying to Nicholas Ridley before they were burned at the stake, "Be of good comfort Master Ridley, and play the man. We shall this day light such a candle by God's grace in England, as (I trust) shall never be put out." It's Jim Elliot writing in his journal, "He is no fool to give what he cannot keep, to gain what he cannot lose."

But character reveals itself in the hidden things of everyday life as well as the dramatic things of public ministry—things like telling the truth when a lie would help you escape trouble, taking the blame when somebody else deserves it, not cutting corners on a job that nobody will inspect, or making unnecessary sacrifices to help people who won't appreciate what you do anyway. Character means living your life before God, fearing only him and seeking to please him alone, no matter how you feel or what others may say and do.

Building character is a difficult process that involves all the experiences of life. "The force of character is cumulative," wrote Emerson in his essay "Self-Reliance." "All the foregone days of virtue work their health into this."

For the Christian, a healthy and holy character is formed by making Scripture a part of our inner being and obeying what it says. It comes from spending time faithfully in worship and prayer, gladly making sacrifices and willingly serving others. Character is strengthened when we suffer and depend on the grace of God to bring us through and glorify his name. It means saying with Job, "But he knows the way that I take; when he has tested me, I shall come forth as gold" (Job 23:10 NKJV). Character comes from discipline and devotion, from courage and commitment, from the myriad of things that Paul experienced and wrote about in 2 Corinthians 6:3–10 and 11:23–12:10.

In this day of media magic, insignificant and ungifted people can be "hyped" into international fame in a short time, but that kind of reputation is no guarantee of character. The British essayist Walter Savage Landor never saw a television set, but he may have had this "false fame" in mind when he wrote over a century ago, "When little men cast long shadows, it is a sign that the sun is setting."

But character is rarely built in solitude; we need the responsibility and accountability that others bring to our lives if character is to be healthy and balanced. Though we don't enjoy the experiences, we need the disappointments and hurts that come with loving and serving people. Whether it's the pastoral staff, a church board, or just the family at home, the relationship of commitment and accountability helps us follow God's blueprint and build a character that pleases him.

The nature of Christian ministry is such that it presents us with daily opportunities that can become either tests to build us up or temptations to tear us down. People trust us and we enter into confidential relationships that can be exploited. Week after week, we stand before people and declare God's Word. Their appreciation can inflate us or their criticism bruise and break us. What we think is success, God may see as failure, while some of our seeming failures may turn out to be our greatest achievements to the glory of God.

Though called to be the servants of all, for the most part, ministers have more freedom than most people to plan their schedules and budget their time. When the pastor tells the secretary he's "going to visit the greens," she's not sure if "greens" has a capital *G* and he's making a house call, or if it's a small *g* and he's heading for the golf course. Depending on the motive and the workload, the minister could participate in either activity to the glory of the Lord; but nobody's standing by to accuse or approve. "In a holy life, there must be control of time," wrote Ralph Turnbull. "We must discipline the hours and bend them to God's purpose."[7]

There is also the dangerous deadening influence of what George Morrison called "an habitual dealing with the outsides of holy things." We mechanically prepare sermons and preach them, but our hearts aren't burning with the message of God. (It may not even be our message. Maybe we "borrowed" it.) Day by day, we pray with hurting people, but each prayer is just like the last one, and nobody knows the difference. The prophet Malachi had this kind of ministry in mind when he denounced the priests of his day who were only hirelings and not shepherds.

If we would only take advantage of them, ministry offers us excellent opportunities to mature in Christian character, to discover and develop our gifts, and to become true people of God. To be able to devote a whole life to studying and teaching God's truth, serving with God's people, bearing burdens, and sharing in the building of the church is quite a privilege! People who waste this opportunity, or who abandon it for something else, usually find out too late what a bad bargain they made.

Like a great cathedral, character is built a day at a time, a stone at a time, with patience and deliberation, all the while seeking to follow God's step-by-step plan. And, like a great cathedral, character can be quietly destroyed, little by little, in many hidden places, unseen even by those who know us best, undetected perhaps by ourselves, but never unnoticed by God. One day the storm blows and the structure crashes, and great is the fall thereof. Then people ask, "What happened?"

The deterioration of character is an "inside job." We drift from God and fall into sin, and then we try to avoid responsibility by blaming others or pleading extenuating circumstances; but the charges won't stand up in God's court. The simple fact is that character erodes because people fail to heed Proverbs 4:23, "Keep your heart with all diligence, for out of it spring the issues of life" (NKJV).[8]

Life is built on character, and character is built on the decisions we make. The daily decisions of life, small and great, cement each stone into the cathedral of character. In defiance of his parents' wishes and God's law, Samson decided to marry a Philistine woman, little realizing his decision was the first step toward a Philistine dungeon. David decided to leave the battlefield and rest at home; and in laying aside his armor, he discovered he couldn't stand against the wiles of the devil or the desires of his own body. On the other hand, people like Joseph and Joshua, Ruth and Esther, and Peter and John decided to trust God and take their stand with God's people, and they were used of God to accomplish exploits.

The erosion of character usually begins with neglect: we stop reading the Word, or worshiping with God's people, or taking time to meditate and pray. We stop giving and start asking, "What will *I* get out of it?" We stop hungering for holiness and exercising spiritual discipline and discernment. We stop making those sacrifices that show our special love for Christ and his people. We do our job mechanically because our heart isn't in it. In time, we find ourselves "making arrangements to sin," convinced that what nobody knows, we can get away with.

The process is deadly: first the drifting, then the secret sinning, then the hidden eroding of character that ultimately leads to the embarrassing public fall. As time goes on, we find it more convenient to sin (we don't have to be tempted; we tempt ourselves) and easier to laugh it off. "It's not really serious," we say to ourselves, "and God understands and forgives."

Along with an unprotected heart, a defiled conscience contributes to the decay of character. Circumstances become boring or painful, so we stop enjoying the good people and the healthy experiences of real life and start looking for substitutes in a fantasy world of our own creation. In our imagination, where nobody can see it, we build our own secret world where *we* have the power and *we* enjoy the success. In this alternate world of the imagination, we satisfy unholy appetites that family and friends would be shocked to discover. We think we can enjoy these sins safely because all this corruption is hidden in our private picture gallery. We forget that every evil thought and imagination tears down character and eventually comes out in the open.

> Sow a thought and you reap an action.
> Sow an action and you reap a character.
> Sow a character and you reap a destiny.

The Foundation of Ministry Is Character

The tragedy is that most people really think they can enjoy a double life and get away with it, that there will be no harvest. In their hypocrisy, they fool others; in their duplicity, they fool themselves; but there's no way they can fool God and change his inexorable laws. "Do not be deceived. God is not mocked; for whatever a man sows, that he will also reap" (Gal. 6:7 NKJV). The truth eventually comes out. "Then, when desire has conceived, it gives birth to sin; and sin, when it is full-grown, brings forth death" (James 1:15 NKJV). The womb of the imagination gives birth to sin; and sin, being a murderer, grows up and starts to kill. Character dies, devotion dies, a happy home dies, a reputation dies, a ministry dies—and perhaps the minister dies too. What could have been a fruitful garden becomes a trash heap and then a graveyard.

Can damaged character be restored and broken ministry be repaired?

No, if the offender offers excuses instead of confession, shows regret instead repentance, resists authority and runs around looking for second and third opinions. No, if the offender rushes into the arms of the nearest false prophet who says "Peace, peace" where there is no peace. No, if the offender enrolls in a thirty-day, surefire rehabilitation program that is neither costly nor painful, supervised by somebody who prefers to whitewash instead of letting God wash white.

But, yes, if the offender is willing to confess sin humbly, judge it severely, turn from it completely, submit obediently, and cooperate patiently as the Potter and his assistants seek to make the vessel again. If the original building process took time and was demanding, the rebuilding process likewise takes time and can be even more demanding; but it can be done.

Should restored offenders be allowed to serve?

Yes, if restoration has been biblical and thorough and if the offender gives evidence of sincerity and humility. The purpose of discipline is *restoration:* ". . . restore him gently. But watch yourself, or you also may be tempted" (Gal. 6:1). The purpose of restoration is *fellowship:* "... you ought to forgive and comfort him, so that he will not be overwhelmed by excessive sorrow" (2 Cor. 2:7).

One purpose of fellowship is *ministry:* "... that there should be no division in the body, but that its parts should have equal concern for each other" (1 Cor. 12:25).

What begins with biblical restoration ought to end in biblical fellowship and service. If the restoration process isn't biblical, then the "fellowship" is spurious and the "ministry" dangerous. The "restored" servant is toxic, not healthy; and whatever ministry ensues will be defiling and destructive.[9]

No true servant of God tries to see how close he or she can come to sin and still remain eligible for service. They respect the words of the psalmist, "Let those who love the LORD hate evil" (Ps. 97:10). And they're mindful of Solomon's counsel, "Guard your heart, for it is the wellspring of life" (Prov. 4:23).

> *It's* easier to build character and guard it than to rebuild it after you've lost it. "Let me be taught that the first great business on earth is the sanctification of my own soul." (Henry Martyn)

Chapter Two

The Nature of Ministry Is Service¹

The congregation couldn't believe what their pastor was saying. Pastor Jim had just returned from a one-day leadership seminar and was sharing what he'd learned. The title of his message was "How Could I Be So Wrong?" and his text was Hebrews 13:17, "Obey those who rule over you, and be submissive."

"I've been your pastor for three years now," he said, "and I've been doing it all wrong. I've been working for you. That's going to change. From now on, you will be the servants and I will be the leader. That's the biblical pattern. It worked for Moses, Joshua, David, and Paul, and it will work for us.

"It's my job to fill the pulpit with preaching and your job to fill the pews with people. It's my job to plan the church program and your job to carry out my plan and pay the bills. We're an army and somebody has to be the general. God has made the pastor the general."

The military metaphor was the wrong one to use. After the service, the saints went marching out like an army, determined to declare war on their pastor. What happened during the next six months was witnessed by the angels and applauded by the demons, but is best left unrecorded among the saints.

He didn't feel an angel nudge him, but for some reason Joe was suddenly wide awake. His first thought was that the phone was going to ring. Joe lay there praying, and then, sure enough, the phone rang. It was Bruce Hibbert's wife with the sad news that her husband had just died.

The phone awakened Midge. "Trouble?" she asked sleepily.

"Nora Hibbert just called. Bruce died of a heart attack a few minutes ago, and I'm going over."

"Do you want me to go with you?" she asked. "Billy's old enough to take care of Jan and Pete for a few hours."

"No, the kids need you here. But just as soon as you can, rally the troops and get people fixing food and doing what they can to help Nora. And please call Phil and cancel our golf game and lunch. Too many important things to do today even if it is my day off."

As Midge drifted off to sleep, in her mind she heard her husband saying what she'd often heard him say when their lives were interrupted: "Remember, dear, we're here to serve. People will remember our kindnesses long after they forget my sermons."

The nature of ministry is service; for Jesus said, "I am among you as one who serves" (Luke 22:27). But what Pastor Jim was exposed to in that high-powered seminar wasn't a theology of Spirit-filled servant leadership; it was a philosophy of ego-centered dictatorship. The ecclesiastical superstar who led the meetings knew very little about how to be a shepherd who leads the sheep for their good and God's glory. He inspired Jim to become a wolf in shepherd's clothing, exploiting the flock to satisfy his own ego, and eventually destroying them.

Nobody should be in Christian ministry who is unwilling to do what Jesus did: put on a towel and become a servant. The sixth-century monk John Climacus wrote, "It is not right for a lion to pasture sheep, and it is not safe for one still tyrannized by the passions to rule over passionate men."[2]

Our English word *minister* comes directly from the Latin and means "a subordinate, a servant, an attendant or assistant." The Romans used it to refer to a house servant, a servant of the gods in the temple, or a public official. There were at least sixty million slaves in the Roman Empire, and slaves were considered nonpeople—merchandise to be sold or discarded like pieces of used furniture. To be a servant was a demeaning thing to the Romans, but Jesus changed all that by his life and death and by his gift of the Holy Spirit to his people. He turned society upside down by proving that a servant's heart is the happiest and freest heart of all.

Several words for "servant" are used in the New Testament and applied to Christian ministry: *oketes,* the household servant; *doulos,* the bond-slave; *huperetes* the under-servant, the subordinate; and *diakonos,* the servant, the attendant or minister. Paul wasn't ashamed to call himself "the bond-slave (*doulos*) of Jesus Christ" (Rom. 1:1; 2 Cor. 4:5; Gal. 1:10; Phil. 1:1; Titus 1:1), and frequently he called himself a *diakonos* (servant) of Jesus Christ (1 Cor. 3:5; 2 Cor. 3:6; 6:4; Eph. 3:7; Col. 1:23). There was no question in Paul's mind that ministers are servants of God and of God's people (". . . ourselves as your servants for Jesus' sake," 2 Cor. 4:5).

John R. W. Stott writes, "The shameful cult of human personalities which tarnished the life of the first century Corinthian church still persists in Christendom, and a most improper and unbecoming regard is paid to some church leaders today."[3] The Presbyterian moderator who introduced J. Hudson Taylor as "our illustrious guest" wasn't prepared for the missionary's quiet response: "Dear friends, I am the little servant of an illustrious Master."[4] Taylor had written in the fourth issue of his magazine *China's Millions,* "All God's giants have been weak men, who did great things for God because they reckoned on His being with them."[5]

One of God's giants was John Wesley. During a single week in July 1757, Wesley preached ten times in eight different towns, traveling by horseback. He wrote in his journal, "I do indeed live by preaching!"[6] He had the right idea, the biblical idea, for true servants of God are nourished by serving. "My food," said Jesus, "is to do the will of him who sent me and to finish his work" (John 4:34).

Perhaps the hardest thing about being a slave was the impossibility of saying "no" to your master. Slaves did what they were told whether they agreed with the assignment or not. But Christ's relationship with his servants isn't like that, for he said, "I no longer call you servants, because a servant does not know his master's business. Instead, I have called you friends, for everything that I learned from my Father I have made known to you" (John 15:15).

It's interesting to note that the servants mentioned in the Gospel of John knew things that other people didn't know. The servants at the Cana wedding knew where the excellent wine came from (John 2:9), and the nobleman's servants knew when the man's son had become well (John 4:51). Although they didn't fully understand all that he taught them, the disciples knew what would occur on that fateful Passover (John 13:19; 14:29). Satan keeps his servants in the dark (Acts 5:7). "The path of the righteous is like the first gleam of dawn, shining ever brighter till the full light of day" (Prov. 4:18).

However, when he gives us an assignment, the Master doesn't always reveal *everything* about it. He does this for at least two reasons: (1) we may not be ready to understand it yet (John 13:7; 16:12), and (2) when we walk by faith, we live on promises, not on explanations. Abraham left home and didn't know where he was going (Heb. 11:8), a practice that would frighten CEOs who must have their five-year plans and their long-range projections. Abraham obediently put his beloved Isaac on the altar, not knowing whether his son would be allowed to live or if he would die and be raised from the dead (Heb. 11:17–19). Jesus served a day at a time, even an hour at a time (John 11:9), and got his orders from the Father each morning (Isa. 50:4–5; Mark 1:35).

The word translated "friends" in John 15:15 means "a king's friends at court." People in authority have always had their inner circle of friends to serve as confidants and loyal helpers; and that is our position at the throne of Jesus Christ, our King.

Like Abraham, "the friend of God" (2 Chron. 20:7; Isa. 41:8, James 2:23), we can share his secrets and by our praying and serving be a part of accomplishing his will on earth (Gen. 18). "The LORD confides in those who fear him; he makes his covenant known to them" (Ps. 25:14).

There are two images of the church in Scripture that best illustrate the kind of servant ministry God's people need: the family and the flock. "We are his people [the family], the sheep of his pasture [the flock]" (Ps. 100:3). If their spiritual growth is as it should be, God's people need loving, spiritual parents and faithful shepherds.

Let's consider what it means for us to minister to the family of God. Both as a missionary evangelist and a pastor, Paul saw himself serving as a *spiritual father.* "I am not writing this to shame you, but to warn you, as my dear children. Even though you have ten thousand guardians in Christ, you do not have many fathers, for in Christ Jesus I became your father through the gospel" (1 Cor. 4:14–15).

It's one thing for people to *believe* in Christ and *enter* the family of God, but quite something else for them to *behave* like Christians and *enjoy* the family of God. The obstetrician and the pediatrician each have important tasks to perform, and the "spiritual parent" often has to do both. One of the tragedies of evangelism is the way professed believers are abandoned instead of assimilated into the church family and nurtured in the Word.

God has ordained that believers grow and serve in a family, with other children of God. This family isn't perfect, but it's God's ordained way to mature his children. The heavenly Father wants his children under the care of spiritual "parents" who can feed them (1 Cor. 3:1–3), discipline them (1 Cor. 4:14–21), and protect them (2 Cor. 11:1–6). "But we were gentle among you, just as a nursing mother cherishes her own children," Paul reminded the new believers in Thessalonica (1 Thess. 2:7 NKJV). Then to balance the picture, he added, "As you know how we exhorted, and comforted, and charged every one of you, as a father does his own children" (1 Thess. 2:11 NKJV).

The image of the nursing mother suggests that Paul shared his own life with these new believers and didn't turn them over to baby-sitters. A nursing mother can't go too far away from her baby if the baby is to be fed, and that feeding is an expression of her own love. Of course, there comes a time when believers must be weaned away from their spiritual instructors and taught to feed themselves (Ps. 131; 1 Cor. 3:1–3; Heb. 5:12–14);[7] but we never outgrow the need for parental love. Parents rejoice as they see their children maturing and helping others mature.

As a spiritual father, Paul took time to teach and encourage his spiritual children *individually* ("every one of you"). The man who wrote the words to "Onward Christian Soldiers," The Reverend Sabine Baring-Gould, was the father of sixteen children, and sometimes he had a difficult time remembering who they were. At a Christmas party, he asked a pretty child, "And whose little girl are you, my dear?" She burst into tears and replied, "I'm yours, Daddy!"[8] Paul didn't have that problem.

Paul not only taught his children, but he set a good example for them as every father should: "You are witnesses, and so is God, of how holy, righteous and blameless we were among you who believed" (1 Thess. 2:10). Children learn far more from what we *do* than from what we *say*, and there's no substitute for a godly example. That's why Paul admonished Timothy in Ephesus to "set an example for the believers in speech, in life, in love, in faith, and in purity" (1 Tim. 4:12).

"A bishop then must be blameless. . . ." (1 Tim. 3:2 NKJV). The root word of "blameless" means "to lay hold of," suggesting that when ministers are "blameless," there's nothing in their lives that anybody can lay hold of to accuse them. Ministers aren't sinless, but they ought to be blameless and above reproach.

Serving as a spiritual parent to a growing church family isn't an easy task, and nobody can do it alone. The members of the family are at different stages of spiritual growth, and some of them have difficulties that demand very special attention. Getting to know the older members individually and integrating the new believers into the family successfully demands prayer, patience, and more time than any minister has available; but with God's help, we must do the best we can and leave the rest with him.

The image of the church as a flock of sheep just doesn't seem to belong to our contemporary world of dynamic megacities and a changing rural population. Most children and young adults in our churches have probably never seen a flock of sheep and have no idea how these animals behave, unless, of course, they happen to see them on television or they meet them in a Christmas display at a shopping mall. "The Lord is my shepherd" is a familiar, sentimental phrase, but to most people it belongs to a faraway world of quaint rural villages surrounded by clean air and green pastures.

But this concept of "backward rural Christianity" isn't accurate. Historian Wayne A. Meeks claims that "within a decade of the crucifixion of Jesus, the village culture of Palestine had been left behind, and the Greco-Roman city became the dominant environment of the Christian movement."[9] In fact, it was to a group of elders from the large and influential city of Ephesus that Paul said, "Keep watch over yourselves and all the flock of which the Holy Spirit has made you overseers. Be shepherds of the church of God, which he bought with his own blood" (Acts 20:28).

Perhaps one reason some churches are in trouble today is their loss of the biblical concept of what they really are. In our noble attempt to be "relevant" in a changing world, we've thoughtlessly abandoned the pastoral image of the shepherd and sheep, and have blindly adopted the corporate image of the pastor as CEO, the elders as a board of directors, and the church family as customers to serve. In so doing, we've quietly changed our expectations of what a minister and a church ought to be and do, which has often led to conflict and pain in churches. In one large denomination alone, over fifty pastors a week are resigning under pressure. One main cause is confusion over how to measure the ministry.

It wasn't an accident that Jesus called himself the Good Shepherd or that he compared his people to a flock of sheep. Call it an antique rural image if you wish, but the image carries with it some practical truths that are desperately needed today. Granted, the flock isn't the only image of the church in the Bible, but it's repeated often enough to make us believe it's significant. If the title "shepherd—pastor" was good enough for Jesus and Paul, it ought to be good enough for us.

To put it plainly, *shepherds serve their sheep.* Shepherds know their sheep and can call them by name. They lead their sheep to places where they can find food, water, and shelter. They protect the sheep from enemies, they apply healing oil when the sheep have been cut or bruised, they enable the sheep to be useful in growing wool, providing milk, and reproducing after their kind. When any of the sheep go astray, the shepherd goes after them and seeks to bring them back.

It doesn't take much imagination to apply this to the local church and the ministry of the pastor and elders. They lead the sheep into the Word of God for spiritual nourishment and refreshment. They keep alert lest Satan's wolves invade the flock (Acts 20:28–31), and they equip the sheep for being useful in the kingdom of God (Eph. 4:11–12). When the sheep stray, the shepherds lovingly go after them (James 5:19–20), and when the sheep hurt, the shepherds apply the medicine of God's Word (Ps. 107:20) to promote healing. Shepherding is a personal ministry, a sacrificial ministry, and a demanding ministry; but it's a rewarding ministry.

However, not every flock enjoys that kind of care. Consider what God said in Ezekiel 34 about the shepherds in the land of Judah.[10] They were selfish and fed themselves and not the flock. They used and abused the flock to get what they wanted, but they didn't minister to the needs of the sheep. The shepherds didn't protect the sheep from enemies and some of the sheep were destroyed. They didn't search for the lost or try to heal the weak and the lame. The sheep were scattered because nobody cared for them.

When Jesus restored Peter to apostleship, he commissioned him to feed the lambs, tend the sheep, and feed the sheep (John 21:15–17). The fisherman became a shepherd. But before he gave that threefold commission, Jesus asked Peter three times, "Simon, do you love me?" *The under-shepherd's love for the Chief Shepherd is the most important part of ministry.* If we love the Good Shepherd, we will love his sheep and minister to them in love. If we don't truly love Jesus Christ, then we'll love ourselves and become selfish shepherds who think only of what others can do for us, not what we can do for others.

Church growth experts have determined that one man can effectively pastor only about 150 people; so, as the flock grows, the shepherd must enlist help.[11] He must be careful that the people who assist him are true shepherds who are looking for opportunities to serve and not just hirelings looking for jobs. But no matter how large the church becomes, a minister must never lose the shepherd's heart. *Loving the people and maintaining the heart of a servant is the basis for all that the pastor does.*

It's really rewarding to watch what happens in a church when a shepherd comes who loves and serves the people, stays with them through thick and thin, and seeks to minister to them to the glory of God. The Holy Spirit begins to create a spirit of unity based on love, and the people almost unconsciously adopt their shepherd's attitude of service as they care for one another. A compassionate, caring congregation reaches out to others, and the church experiences growth in grace and in numbers. It's not the result of religious "hype" or clever leadership techniques; it's the result of the Holy Spirit working deep within the hearts of the people because of the ministry of the Word of God and prayer.

In time, of course, the critics and disgruntled members feel ill at ease in this climate of renewal and decide to find churches where the atmosphere is less threatening to their low level of impersonal Christian profession. Of course, when they leave their excuse is that "the church isn't spiritual anymore"; but what they're really saying is that the church is too spiritual for their brand of Christianity. They want to be spectators, not servants; they want to hold offices, but not use the offices to serve God and the people; they want to be important, but not involved. The shepherd gets the blame, of course, but no matter; the Spirit of God is at work, Jesus is being glorified, and that's all that really counts.

> *The mark of the true servant of God is a towel and not a scepter. He serves Christ by serving his people. "Whatever you did for one of the least of these brothers of mine, you did for Me" (Matt. 25:40).*

Chapter Three

The Motive of Ministry Is Love

The saintly Scottish preacher Andrew Bonar listened to a well-known preacher proclaim the Word, and after the meeting approached the speaker and said, "You love to preach, don't you?"

"Yes, I do," the famous preacher replied.

Then Bonar asked, "Do you love the men to whom you preach?"[1]

Love for the sheep begins with love for the Shepherd who died to save them (John 10:11) and lives to perfect them (Heb. 13:20–21). Before he commissioned Peter to care for his sheep, Jesus asked him three times, "Do you love me?" (John 21:15–17). The question was both appropriate and penetrating and is applicable to us today. If we don't love the Shepherd, how can we love his sheep?

In 1757, John Newton, composer of "Amazing Grace," wrote to the celebrated evangelist George Whitefield:

> The longer I live, the more I see of the vanity and the sinfulness of our unchristian disputes; they eat up the very vitals of religion. I grieve to think of how often I have lost my time and my temper in that way, in presuming to regulate the vineyards of others, when I have neglected my own. . . . When our dear Lord questioned Peter,

after his fall and recovery, he said not, Art thou wise, learned and eloquent? nay, he said not, Art thou clear and sound, and orthodox? But this only, "Lovest thou me?" An answer to this was sufficient then; why not now?[2]

The servant of the Lord can't minister effectively if mixed motives compete in the heart. Love of attention and praise, love of money, love of authority, even love of ministry, can never glorify God or carry God's servant through the hills and valleys of spiritual service. Only a love for Christ can do that. "For the love of Christ constrains us," Paul testified (2 Cor. 5:14 NKJV). Whether the apostle meant Christ's love for him or his own love for Christ is unimportant since the two go together. "We love him because he first loved us" (1 John 4:19 NKJV).

David, a faithful shepherd, was a man after God's own heart, especially in his attitude toward his people. When Israel was being chastened because of David's sin, the king cried out to the Lord, "Surely I have sinned, and I have done wickedly; but these sheep, what have they done?" (2 Sam. 24:17 NKJV). The heart of a true shepherd shows up when his people suffer, and the shepherd isn't ashamed to reveal it.

"Do you love me?" isn't one of the routine questions asked by a moderator at an ordination examination. But it's the key question asked by the Master, who so loves his sheep that he doesn't want to put them into the hands of hirelings who will abandon them or false shepherds who will exploit them. "If the love of Christ constrain you," said Charles Spurgeon, "it will make you love others, for his was love to others, love to those who could do him no service, who deserved nothing at his hands."[3]

The more we love Christ, the more our hearts will be filled with his love; and that love must be shared with others. To quote Spurgeon again: "The love of Christ was a practical love. He did not love in thought only and in word, but in deed and in truth, and if the love of Christ constraineth us we shall throw our souls into the work and service of love."[4]

Our Lord shall have the last word: "Whoever has my commands and obeys them, he is the one who loves me. He who loves me will be loved by my Father, and I too will love him and show myself to him. . . . If anyone loves me, he will obey my teaching. My Father will love him, and we will come to him and make our home with him" (John 14:21, 23 NIV).

"Ministry love" isn't something we manufacture. Actors can psych themselves up to play their roles, but shepherds need something deeper to fulfill their calling. Before each performance, the great illusionist Howard Thurston repeated to himself just before the curtain opened, "I love my audience! I love my audience!" That approach may work for magicians, but it won't succeed when it comes to caring for sheep. If the servants of God are to love people, both believers and unbelievers, they must see people as Jesus sees them and respond as he would respond. No amount of psychology can accomplish this; it has to come from the Spirit of God. "God has poured out his love into our hearts by the Holy Spirit, whom he has given us" (Rom. 5:5 NIV).

Why must the love of Christ motivate us in ministry? For one thing, we can't represent Christ, the loving Shepherd, if we ourselves are lacking in love. "Ministry takes place when divine resources meet human needs through loving channels to the glory of God."[5] If that definition is true, then at least two motives are involved in true Christian ministry: glorifying God and loving God. Philanthropy can meet human needs, but only Christian ministry can share God's love and glorify God's great name. It's doubtful that we can glorify God's name if we aren't moved by his love.

Something else is true: without a love for the people we serve, ministry becomes drudgery. We become like Jonah, who did his work reluctantly because he didn't want another spanking; or we act like the elder brother in Christ's parable (Luke 15:11–32), who did his father's work but didn't share his father's loving heart. The elder brother had his own hidden agenda, and when his plans were disappointed he became angry and absented himself from the feast. Both Jonah and the elder brother were angry servants, which is often the tragic consequence of service without love. Ministry motivated by love will build you up (1 Cor. 8:1), but ministry motivated only by obligation or duty can produce hidden anger and eventually tear you down.

Loving ministry not only builds up the servants, but it also builds up the people we serve. The servant who looks at people and asks, "What can they do for me?" will end up exploiting them instead of serving them. The prophet Ezekiel had this kind of shepherd in mind when he wrote:

> Woe to the shepherds[6] of Israel who feed themselves! Should not the shepherds feed the flock? You eat the fat and clothe yourselves with the wool; you slaughter the fatlings, but you do not feed the flock. The weak you have not strengthened, nor have you healed those who were sick, nor bound up the broken, nor brought back what was driven away, nor sought what was lost; but with force and cruelty you have ruled them. So they were scattered because there was no shepherd. (Ezek. 34:2–5 NKJV)

Sheep can be led but not driven, and experienced shepherds know that it requires a great deal of patience to lead the flock. Not all the sheep will follow at the same pace or keep as close to the shepherd as they should, and some sheep will carelessly stray and have to be sought by the shepherd and brought back to the safety of the flock. Shepherds know their sheep and can call them by name, and they will follow. Shepherding demands patience, but "love is patient, love is kind" (1 Cor. 13:4 NIV).

A pastor visited a farm family where the children were raising two sheep, with hopes of winning some ribbons at the local fair. The children were at camp that week, so their father was left to take care of the precious animals.

"Let's do the chores," he said to his pastor, and together they put fresh hay in the mangers and clean water in the bowls. "Now we'll take the sheep for a walk to tone up their muscles," he announced; and together they led the sheep out, each animal on a halter. The sheep followed, but not for long. The first one dropped to the ground and wouldn't budge, and the second one followed his example. The men had to put the sheep back on their feet, but the animals still wouldn't walk, so the farmer put them back in their pen. As he stood staring at them, the man said quietly, "Pastor, now you know why the Bible calls God's people sheep."

When Jesus looked at the crowds, he was moved with compassion because he saw them "as sheep not having a shepherd" (Matt. 9:36). They want their own way, not God's way; yet they desperately need spiritual leaders to guide them. The people Jesus loved are those you and I might be tempted to avoid. But if we did, what would happen to them—*and what would happen to us?* It isn't enough for the church to proclaim "God loves you!" if Christians don't demonstrate that love personally. This love must begin with the shepherd.

Can people really know that we love them?

Yes, most of them can. To begin with, if we really love people, we accept them as they are and identify with their deepest needs. This doesn't mean we approve of their lifestyle or whitewash their record, for Christian love is neither blind nor hypocritical (Phil. 1:9–11). The most unloving thing we can do to people is to close our eyes to their greatest needs and carry on a masquerade ministry that's based on illusion. No, Christian love means seeing saints and sinners as they are, but seeing them as people for whom Christ died and in whom Christ can do wonderful new things. Without ignoring the problem, we see the potential. As Jesus said to Simon, so we say to them: "You are . . . You will be. . . ." (John 1:42 NIV).

When we're controlled by the love of Christ, we "speak the truth in love" (Eph. 4:15). It's well been said that truth without love is brutality, but love without truth is hypocrisy. God's servants don't want to be guilty of either sin. To be able to confront a lost sinner or an erring believer with this kind of love is to minister as Jesus ministered. Jesus saw the cancer of covetousness in the heart of the rich young ruler, but he loved him and sought to deliver him (Mark 10:21). Our Lord even saw the treachery in the heart of Judas, and humbly washed his feet.

Love doesn't ask, "Do they deserve my help?" It just goes ahead and helps. (Did we deserve what Jesus did for us?) "Love is patient, love is kind" (1 Cor. 13:4 NIV). Love doesn't give up on people, no matter how far they may have strayed from God. Love sacrifices and serves when the sacrifice and service are neither acknowledged nor appreciated. Love returns good for evil, healing for hurting, and blessing for cursing. Love transforms us from reservoirs into channels and enables us to say, "What's mine is yours; I'll share it." Love won't let us pass by on the other side the way the priest and Levite did, pretending that hurting people don't exist. Love enables us to be good Samaritans who go where people are and do what we can to help them (Luke 10:30–37).

Love listens and doesn't interrupt, and then responds with healing words of truth. What we hear may be foolish, hateful, even blasphemous; but we don't reply in kind. "Being reviled, we bless; being persecuted, we endure it; being defamed, we entreat" (1 Cor. 4:12–13 NKJV). "Blessed are you when they revile and persecute you, and say all kinds of evil against you falsely for my sake," Jesus told his disciples. "Rejoice and be exceedingly glad, for great is your reward in heaven, for so they persecuted the prophets who were before you" (Matt. 5:11–12 NKJV).

A prayer of St. Ignatius Loyola summarizes the kind of ministry we've been describing:

> To give and not to count the cost;
> To fight and not to heed the wounds;
> To toil and not to seek for rest;
> To labor and not to look for any reward
> Save that of knowing that I do Thy will.

Sometimes it's easier to love the sinners than it is to love the saints, as the familiar rhyme puts it:

> To live above with saints we love
> Will certainly be glory.
> To live below with saints we know—
> That's another story!

One reason, of course, is that we expect more from God's people than we do from the world's crowd, and God's people expect more from us. It takes a diamond to cut a diamond; but if we depend on God's grace, the abrasiveness of the saints can make us into more beautiful jewels. What Joseph said to his brothers is effective medicine for a minister's hurting heart: "You intended to harm me, but God intended it for good" (Gen. 50:20 NIV). That statement is a patriarchal version of Romans 8:28, and it works.

Yes, the saints can be trying and taxing. More than once our Lord was grieved over his chosen twelve because of their unbelief, their hardness of heart, their vindictive spirit, and their intense competition to be "the greatest." "O unbelieving and perverse generation, how long shall I be with you and put up with you?" (Luke 9:41). The servant isn't above the master; if people grieved him, they will grieve us.

But the fumbling apostles, with the exception of Judas Iscariot, turned out to be mighty servants of the Lord. Almost every pastor, teacher, and missionary can bear witness to the fact that it's often the people we want to give up on who one day become model Christians and effective workers. Why? Because somebody loved them into the will of God. Love "always trusts, always hopes, always perseveres" (1 Cor. 13:7 NIV). The Living Bible paraphrases it: "If you love someone you will be loyal to him no matter what the cost. You will always believe in him, always expect the best of him, and always stand your ground in defending him." A great challenge, but then we have a great God who has shared his great love with us!

If you think the people you're ministering to are difficult and irritating, get better acquainted with the people to whom Paul sent his letters. The believers in Rome had a tough time overcoming their racial prejudices and accepting one another. The church in Corinth was divided four ways. The saints were taking each other to court, getting drunk at the Lord's Supper, and proudly tolerating wickedness in their assembly. People in the Galatian assemblies were "biting and devouring one another" (Gal. 5:15). Some of the Christians in Thessalonica quit their jobs and were sitting around waiting for the Lord to return while they sponged off their hardworking Christian friends.

As Paul dealt with these matters, he was tough-minded but tenderhearted. His purpose was always the same: "warning every man and teaching every man in all wisdom, that we may present every man perfect in Christ Jesus" (Col. 1:28 NKJV). Paul wept and prayed, pleaded and exhorted, while daily facing "the pressure of my concern for all the churches" (2 Cor. 11:28 NIV). "To be a true minister to men," said Phillips Brooks, "is always to accept new happiness and new distress, both of them forever deepening and entering into closer and more inseparable union with each other the more profound and spiritual ministry becomes."[7]

Higher heights of joy and deeper depths of sorrow—that's the landscape of Christian ministry. But the servants don't complain because they do it out of love for the Master.

Having said all this about love, we issue this caveat: our love for saints and sinners must be governed by our love for God and his truth. Why? Because in Christian service we constantly face the danger of our hearts becoming marshmallows and our spines becoming spaghetti, and what ought to be strong love gradually becomes shallow sentiment.

Sentiment has been defined as "feeling without responsibility," but the responsibility of love cannot be abdicated. Christian love is not just an emotional thing; it involves the giving of the whole person to Christ and to others. "Ourselves your servants for Jesus' sake" (2 Cor. 4:5 KJV). Christian love is an act of the will as much as an expression of the heart. We choose to treat others the way God treats us. God listens to us, so we listen to others. God forgives us, so we forgive others. Whether we feel like it or not, we act toward others as Jesus would have acted.

Sometimes this involves what modern counselors are calling "tough love." The Bible calls it "chastening" or "discipline." Proverbs 3:11–12 is the basic text and Hebrews 12:1–13 is the exposition. "My son, do not despise the LORD's discipline and do not resent his rebuke, because the LORD disciplines those he loves, as a father the son he delights in" (Prov. 3:11–12 NIV).

Joseph exercised tough love in the way he handled his brothers and patiently brought them to confession and repentance. Moses exercised tough love in the way he forced the Israelites to face their sins after they made and worshiped the golden calf. God manifested tough love in the steps he took to restore David after he had committed adultery. The prodigal son's father showed tough love by staying home and not rushing to the faraway country to rescue his son.

Tough love knows that there's a difference between *hurting* people and *harming* people. "Faithful are the wounds of a friend, but the kisses of an enemy are deceitful" (Prov. 27:6 NKJV). On occasion medical doctors hurt us, but they rarely, if ever, harm us. David kissed Absalom when he should have disciplined him (2 Sam. 14:33); but Joseph first disciplined his brothers, then he kissed them (Gen. 45:14–15).

Scriptures such as Matthew 18:15–35, Romans 16:17–20, 1 Corinthians 5, and 2 Thessalonians instruct us to exercise tough love as we minister to God's people. As every loving parent knows, discipline is never easy, but it is essential for the good of those for whom we are responsible. "You who love the LORD, hate evil!" (Ps. 97:10 NKJV). "Seek good, not evil. . . . Hate evil, love good" (Amos 5:14–15).

The motive for ministry is love. Ministry would be much easier if all we had to do was obey a set of regulations, but then we would never mature or be able to help others mature. God's goal for his church is "the measure of the stature of the fullness of Christ" (Eph. 4:14 KJV), and to reach toward that goal requires love. "But speaking the truth in love, [we] may grow up into him in all things, which is the head, even Christ" (Eph. 4:15 KJV).

*T*he most sensitive thing in ministry is a shepherd's heart. If you have it, don't lose it; if you don't have it, ask God to give it to you, no matter what the cost.

Chapter Four

The Measure of Ministry Is Sacrifice

"Well, we've lasted three years," Ray said to Phyllis as they drove home from church. "According to the sacred seminary statistics, if we last two more years we're in for a long ministry here in Drexel Park."

Phyllis was silent for a time, and then said, "But one thing bothers me."

"What's that?"

"These first three years have been too easy. I have a feeling that something is about to happen to us."

"Too easy!" exclaimed Ray. "Phyllis, we've both worked hard these three years. Sometimes Kenny and Kim thought they were orphans!"

"I don't mean hard work, Ray," Phyllis said quietly. "I mean sacrifice. It hasn't really cost us anything. Anybody can work hard at a job, but this isn't a job. It's *ministry*, and ministry always demands something more."

Ray pondered her words. "Okay, then let's agree with each other—and with the Lord—that when we meet the crosses and go into the furnaces, we're not going to run away. If we're called to sacrifice, let's at least not waste our suffering."

Phyllis turned out to be right. In a few months, the atmosphere of their lives changed from sunshine to intermittent clouds and storms.

The first rumbles of thunder were heard at the annual church business meeting when the finance chairman announced that the budget wouldn't allow Ken and Phyllis to attend the denominational conference. "It's only a vacation anyway," he said, trying to be funny, "and we need the money for more important things." The rumbling got louder when he said, "There will be no staff raises this year. We just can't afford it." (It upset Ken when he saw so many heads nod in agreement.)

A week later, the rain started to fall when Kim was diagnosed a juvenile diabetic. She spent nearly a week in the hospital to get her chemistry balanced and then returned home carrying some rather expensive equipment that she would use for the rest of her life. Phyllis picked up some cookbooks for diabetics and Kenny began complaining that they wouldn't have any more desserts. "Why didn't she catch something else, like leprosy?" he grumbled. "At least lepers can eat pie and cake!"

"This household is now in 'depression mode,'" Ray announced at dinner one evening. "We're following the 'depression slogan' my grandfather quoted to me when I was growing up: 'Use it up, wear it out; make it do or do without.' We're not going to lack anything we really need, but we may not get all the things we'd like to have."

In the months that followed, Phyllis watched the budget carefully and she and Ray went without so the children could have what they needed (and even a few things they didn't need). Ray paid more than one ministry expense out of his own pocket, including attending the annual conference. He and Phyllis took congregational pressures and criticisms graciously ("If she'd feed those children a balanced diet, that girl wouldn't be a diabetic!").

The family went out for a special Sunday dinner to celebrate their fifth anniversary at the church. During the meal, Ray said, "Phyllis, I wish you weren't such a successful prophetess. These past two years have been the toughest of our whole married life and our entire ministry."

Phyllis smiled. "But we've learned and grown a lot. By God's grace, we weathered the storm successfully and we're stronger and happier because of the sacrifices we made. Best of all, serving the church isn't just a job. It's a ministry."

"Preaching that costs nothing accomplishes nothing," said John Henry Jowett. "If the study is a lounge, the pulpit will be an impertinence."[1]

Jowett's statement could be expanded to read: "*Ministry* that costs nothing accomplishes nothing. If the minister's life is without a measure of pain and sacrifice, his ministry will be without blessing." When the going is tough, the hireling runs to easier pastures; but the true shepherd stays with the flock, sacrifices for them, and counts it a privilege to do so.

Of course, those who advocate a different approach to ministry smile at the very mention of sacrifice. They're anxious to hand God's wounded warriors books and cassettes that explain the easy route from earth to heaven, a route that wasn't taken by Jesus or any of the heroes of the faith mentioned in Scripture or in church history. Nowhere in their modern course on "Pastoral Work Made Easy" do you find quoted "You therefore must endure hardship as a good soldier of Jesus Christ" (2 Tim. 2:3 NKJV) or "We must through much tribulation enter into the kingdom of God" (Acts 14:22 KJV).

Every servant of God lives in one of two verses: "For to me, to live is Christ, and to die is gain" (Phil. 1:21 NKJV) or "For all seek their own, not the things which are of Christ Jesus" (Phil. 2:21 NKJV). Moses was willing to die in order to save Israel from God's judgment (Exod. 32:30–35), and Paul was willing to be accursed if it would mean salvation for his people (Rom. 9:1–3). In fact, Paul was even willing to stay out of heaven in order to serve the churches (Phil. 1:19–24)!

The faithful servant of God doesn't deliberately seek trials and pain just to brag about his scars, nor does he make sacrifices in order to earn some future blessing. A commercial attitude toward ministry is dangerous. "See," said Peter, "we have left all and followed you. Therefore, what shall we have?" (Matt. 19:27 NKJV).

Our Lord's reply to Peter was the parable of the laborers in the vineyard (Matt. 20:1–16). The key to the parable is the fact that the men hired early in the morning *insisted on a contract* so they'd know what they would get (vv. 2, 13–14). They got what they asked for, but the other laborers received far more because they let the master decide on the wages. Whenever we insist on a contract from the Lord, we always rob ourselves of the good things he plans for us. Peter finally learned this lesson and moved from "What shall we get?" to "What I do have I give you" (Acts 3:6 NKJV).

The late Henri J. M. Nouwen asked, "What does it mean to be a minister in our contemporary society?" His answer is biblical: "a wounded healer."[2] Unless we've felt the wounds ourselves and experienced God's healing, we can't adequately minister to others who are wounded. God "comforts us in all our tribulation, that we may be able to comfort those who are in any trouble, with the comfort with which we ourselves are comforted by God. For as the sufferings of Christ abound in us, so our consolation also abounds through Christ" (2 Cor. 1:4–5 NKJV).

What are the things that wound the servants of the Lord and call them to suffering and sacrifice? Some of the experiences Paul lists in his Corinthian letters (1 Cor. 4:9–13; 9:19–27; 2 Cor. 4:7–18; 6:1–10; 11:23–12:10) are foreign to most ministers today, unless they are pioneer missionaries, but we do find ourselves identifying with several of them:

- working hard and not being appreciated
- being slandered and having no opportunity to defend ourselves
- being misunderstood but not allowed to explain
- facing perplexity and not knowing where to turn
- "sorrowful, yet always rejoicing"

• sleepless nights and toil-filled days; and "besides everything else," facing daily the pressure of our loving concern for God's people.

The job description isn't too inviting, but the Chief Shepherd doesn't revise it for each applicant.

In addition, pastors are rarely, if ever, satisfied with what they are or how they minister, and their hearts break because of the blindness of people who close their eyes to the church's opportunities. It is easy to understand how ministry can wear people out. We're tempted to say with the Master, "How long shall I stay with you? How long shall I put up with you?" (Matt. 17:17); but we know even as we say it that we'll stay where we are as long as he wants us to stay.

Sometimes the seeming absence of spiritual fruit burdens our hearts, even though we know that we will reap "in due season" if we don't give up (Gal. 6:9). Dr. V. Raymond Edman used to remind the students at Wheaton College, "It's always too soon to quit"; and yet even Moses felt he'd rather die than go on serving a nation of critics, and more than once Jeremiah poured his heart out to God and considered resigning. Jesus set his face like flint as he went to Jerusalem, even though he knew that a cross stood at the end of his journey (Luke 9:51), and Paul turned a deaf ear to the repeated pleas of his friends that he not go to Jerusalem. "But none of these things move me," he told the Ephesian elders, "nor do I count my life dear to myself, so that I may finish my race with joy, and the ministry which I received from the Lord Jesus, to testify to the gospel of the grace of God" (Acts 20:24 NKJV).

A life to live, a race to run, a ministry to fulfill, a message to share. That's what kept Paul going, and it ought to be sufficient to keep us going.

Unless we want to be comfortable hirelings and forfeit God's heavenly approval and reward, there is no easy way to serve the Lord. Ministry involves sacrifice, just as parenthood involves sacrifice, although most parents confess that they're happy to pay the price to meet their children's needs. In the long run, the way we handle sacrifice is a test of character, revealing whether we're serving others or serving ourselves, living for the eternal or the temporal. The shepherd who looks for greener pastures when there's a price to pay right where he is confesses that he knows little about "Calvary love."

An old school chum expressed to Samuel Johnson the thought that the ministry was an easy way to make a living. "Sir, the life of a parson, of a conscientious clergyman, is not easy," said Johnson. "No, Sir, I do not envy a clergyman's life as an easy life, nor do I envy the clergyman who makes it an easy life."[3]

Johnson was a God-fearing man who read his New Testament in the original Greek and took seriously the stewardship of life and the awesomeness of death. He had a special reverence for the ministerial office, and his last statement reveals his spiritual insight. He knew that the minister who contrives an easy life is likely to experience a difficult death as he contemplates facing his Master and giving account. "For we must all appear before the judgment seat of Christ," Paul declares. "Since, then, we know what it is to fear the Lord, we try to persuade men" (2 Cor. 5:10–11).

Ministerial life and service are not without their joys, but the joy of the Lord is always tempered by the fear of the Lord. "Serve the LORD with fear, and rejoice with trembling" (Ps. 2:11 NKJV). We are Christ's servants, but we are also his friends (John 15:14–15); both relationships are important. As servants, we obey him, but it's willing obedience as a friend and not the blind obedience of a slave.

"I have called you friends," said Jesus, "for all things that I heard from my Father I have made known to you" (John 15:15 NKJV). This privileged relationship brings with it a solemn responsibility. Campbell Morgan put it succinctly: "Let us gladden His heart by such intimate friendship that through us He may be able to do what He desires to do for this sad and needy world."[4]

God balances suffering with glory. He doesn't *replace* suffering with glory; rather, he *transforms* suffering into glory. Peter had a hard time understanding this truth and tried to dissuade Jesus when he spoke about going to the cross to die (Matt. 16:21–28). Jesus rebuked Peter and told him he was thinking like the unconverted world and, even worse, working for the devil. It wasn't until his experience on the Mount of Transfiguration that Peter learned that Christ brings glory out of suffering (Matt. 17:1–8), and then he wrote about it in his two epistles. There was nothing glorious about a Roman cross *until Jesus willingly died on one,* and that transformed the cross forever.

In hell, there is suffering but no glory; in heaven, there is glory but no suffering. It's while we're here on earth that we experience both suffering and glory *if we suffer in the will of God and seek to honor him.* Again, Peter is the authority on the subject: "But may the God of all grace, who called us to his eternal glory by Christ Jesus, after you have suffered a while, perfect,[5] establish, strengthen, and settle you" (1 Peter 5:10 NKJV).

We are called by God's grace, called to God's glory, and called to suffer as God's servants. But if we depend on God's grace and live for God's glory, that suffering works for us and not against us. Suffering plus grace produces character and spiritual maturity, glory to God today and glory with God forever.

Too often we're like the two Emmaus disciples who walked the road of defeat and discouragement because they didn't understand the relationship between suffering and glory. "Did not the Christ have to suffer these things and then enter his glory?" asked Jesus. Then he took them through the Old Testament Scriptures and showed them there both the cross and the crown (Luke 24:25–27). Our Lord's wounds from Calvary were not removed at the resurrection; they were glorified.

Just as it's wrong to try to escape suffering by disobeying God's will, it's also wrong to rush impetuously into suffering out of God's will. Jesus lived on a divine timetable and took no unnecessary risks (John 4:1–3; 7:1; 10:39–40; 11:54), a good example for us to follow. He was careful in dealing with his enemies as he answered their questions and accusations, and he admonished his disciples to be "shrewd as snakes and innocent as doves" (Matt. 10:16). This doesn't suggest compromise, but it does call for gentleness and wisdom. "And a servant of the Lord must not quarrel but be gentle to all, able to teach, patient, in humility correcting those who are in opposition" (2 Tim. 2:24–25 NKJV).

Jesus compared his own sacrifice and service to the planting of a seed. "I tell you the truth, unless a kernel of wheat falls to the ground and dies, it remains only a single seed. But if it dies, it produces many seeds" (John 12:24 NIV). In the parable of the tares, Jesus compared God's children to seeds which he, the wise sower, planted wherever he pleased in this world. "The field is the world," but ours is not to weigh the options and look for the perfect place of ministry. Ours is to surrender to the Sower and bear fruit wherever he plants us.

There can be no life without death; there can be no fruit bearing without seed planting. Seeds live for the future: first the suffering, then the glory. Even our Lord couldn't escape yielding to this divine principle. "Whoever serves me must follow me; and where I am, my servant also will be. My Father will honor the one who serves me" (John 12:26).

If the measure of ministry is sacrifice, then the minister who wants to please God has several responsibilities when it comes to suffering.

Expect it. "Dear friends, do not be surprised at the painful trial you are suffering, as though something strange were happening to you" (1 Peter 4:12 NIV). "If the world hates you, you know that it hated Me before it hated you.... If they persecuted me, they will also persecute you" (John 15:18, 20 NKJV).

Accept it as God's gift. "For to you it has been granted on behalf of Christ, not only to believe in him, but also to suffer for his sake" (Phil. 1:29 NKJV).

Evaluate it and yield to God's purposes. "But he knows the way that I take; when he has tested me, I will come forth as gold" (Job 23:10 NIV).

Learn to live a day at a time and to give your cares to him. "Praise be to the Lord, to God our Savior, who daily bears our burdens" (Ps. 68:19 NIV). "Casting all your care upon him, for he cares for you" (1 Peter 5:7 NKJV).

Trust God to turn assigned suffering into eternal glory. "For our light affliction, which is but for a moment, is working for us a far more exceeding and eternal weight of glory" (2 Cor. 4:17 NKJV).

> *Sacrifice is not paying a price. It's making an eternal investment with guaranteed dividends.*

Chapter Five

The Authority of Ministry Is Submission

*E*xactly and precisely, young man, what is your philosophy of ministry?" asked George Larkin, chairman of First Church's pastoral search committee.

Stuart looked at the chairman, sitting straight and alert at the head of the conference table. He sent a quick prayer up to the Lord and replied quietly from the words of 2 Corinthians 4:5: "For we do not preach ourselves, but Jesus Christ as Lord, and ourselves as your servants for Jesus' sake."

"That's *Paul's* answer," said the chairman. "I want *your* answer." His tone was very authoritarian, and Stuart understood why one of the deacons had privately warned him about the chairman. "He's an old military man," said the deacon. "All veterans aren't like that, but he thinks everything should be run like an army. He'll probably expect you to salute when you meet him. He's driven away some of our best people."

"Paul's answer *is* my answer," said Stuart, "and has been since the Lord called me thirteen years ago. Christians are to serve one another and a lost world, and Jesus Christ alone is Lord.

The pastor is the servant who serves the Lord by serving and leading the servants. His authority comes from the Lord."

George pursed his lips. "Doesn't his authority come from the church? After all, we do elect officers and have a chain of command."

"If the church calls me, they'll be acknowledging that Jesus Christ, the Head of the church, has put me here," Stuart answered. "We're all accountable to the Lord and to one another as together we serve Christ. If people are submitted to the Lord, they'll have no problem submitting to one another in the fear of God, as Paul wrote in Ephesians 5:21. And as for a chain of command, we all belong to each other, influence each other, and need each other. I don't see leadership so much as 'command' as compassion and cooperation."

There was a murmur of assent from several of the committee members, but it was quickly silenced by a critical glance from the chairman. The question he obviously wanted to ask but didn't dare was: Will you or will you not do what you are told?

Then the treasurer spoke up. "George, I think we've heard enough to convince us that Pastor Kreider has the right attitude toward the work of the ministry. First Church has had all sorts of pastors. Some were peacocks, some were puppets, and some were petty dictators. It might be refreshing to have a pastor with the heart of a servant, and Pastor Kreider seems to fit the job description."

Stuart smiled and said, "I hope so. One of my professors used to remind us that a pastor must be a servant who leads and a leader who serves. That's my desire and my only desire."

First Church called Stuart to be their pastor; but what to Stuart was a call to serve was to George Larkin a call to arms.

"I guess every church has its Diotrephes,"[1] Stuart said to his wife. "Well, the Lord brought us here, and the battle is the Lord's. Come what may, I'll preach and pray and plug away!"

Ever since the fall of Satan, two wills have been at war in this universe, expressed in two opposite philosophies. The world's philosophy is: take care of number one, even if you have to walk on people to do it. The Christian's philosophy is (or ought to be): submit to God's authority, be a servant, and expect to be occasionally walked on by others. Lucifer took the first route and became Satan, the enemy of God; Jesus took the second route and became the suffering servant of God who today is the exalted King of kings.

Authority is important to the welfare of nations, organizations, homes, and individuals. Without some kind of authority, we would all be horribly mired in anarchy. The young artist develops his or her talent by submitting to authority, listening, watching, and learning. Successful athletes yield to the skill and wisdom of their coaches and do what they're told. The godly Christian submits to the authority of Jesus Christ and the spiritual leaders of the church and seeks to build the church by being a servant.

But submission is not subjugation or slavery. Submission is a voluntary surrender to authority, and it's motivated by love and not fear. Subjugated slaves lose their individuality and become pieces of furniture to be bought and sold. However, submitted Christians, yielded to the Lord, develop their individuality and become more like the Master, developing into the kind of people God has planned for them to be. The people who refuse to submit to God's authority will never really discover who they are and what God wants them to do. No matter how successful they may be in the eyes of the world, unless they change they will be failures in the eyes of God.

When the world's philosophy of leadership starts to infect the church, the abuse of authority is the result. Lucifer and Diotrephes rear their ugly heads. What ought to be a united family becomes a divided army, and the harvest field turns into a battlefield. Time that the church leaders should be investing in ministry is wasted in digging trenches and defending territorial rights. It's all a matter of pride and fear, with adults acting like children and saying, "What's mine is mine! I'll keep it!"

They should be saying, "What's mine is God's gift to me, so I'll share it."

The sad thing is that the peace-loving pastor too often finds himself caught between the trenches and getting shot at from both sides. In personal ministry and from the pulpit he seeks to encourage Christian maturity, but he has to confess with the psalmist, "I am for peace; but when I speak, they are for war" (Ps. 120:7 NKJV).

Along with the Word of God and prayer, the pastor's example of submission and service is perhaps the most valuable spiritual weapon he has for disarming the enemy, calming the conflict, and eventually emptying the trenches. Neither the devil nor his human helpers know quite what to do with Christlike servants who risk the dangers of the battlefield to bring aid to the wounded, leadership to the godly, and love to everybody, "always carrying about in the body the dying of the Lord Jesus, that the life of Jesus also may be manifested in our body" (2 Cor. 4:10 NKJV).

While the insights of "conflict resolution" are helpful and can be used profitably, the concerned shepherd/soldier knows that the first step toward victory is *his own submission to the Lord and to his people.* "And a servant of the Lord must not quarrel but be gentle to all, able to teach, patient, in humility correcting those who are in opposition, if God perhaps will grant them repentance, so that they may know the truth" (2 Tim. 2:24–25 NKJV). In matters of leadership, gentleness is not weakness; it's power under control, power directed toward healing people and not harming them.

It's unfortunate that some church leaders start acting like children whenever they think somebody is threatening their territory or trying to take away their toys. Perhaps that's why the Lord led Paul to use the word *paideuo* ("correcting") in 2 Timothy 2:25, since it refers to the training of a child. After all, the church is a family, and one of the secrets of successful pastoral leadership is to treat church people like members of the family. "Do not rebuke an older man harshly" Paul wrote, "but exhort him as if he were your father. Treat younger men as brothers, older women as mothers, and younger women as sisters, with absolute purity" (1 Tim. 5:1–2).

When we submit to the Lord and make ourselves available for him to use us as he wishes, the burden of the ministry then rests upon him, and we can trust him with ourselves and our future. "We give no offense in anything, that our ministry may not be blamed," is the way Paul described it. "But in all things we commend ourselves as ministers of God: in much patience, in tribulations, in needs, in distresses . . . by purity, by knowledge, by longsuffering, by kindness, by the Holy Spirit, by sincere love" (2 Cor. 6:3–4, 6 NKJV). Paul was simply practicing the lordship of Jesus Christ in his life, a costly experience, but a very necessary one for the building of the church.

Pilots who submit to the authority of the laws of aerodynamics can successfully fly their planes. Scientists who obey the basic laws of chemistry and physics will keep from destroying themselves and others. Physicians who submit to the laws that govern medical science and the functions of the human body will promote health and well-being. Submit to God's laws and they work for you; oppose them and they work against you.

What's true in the natural realm is also true in the spiritual realm. Ministers who submit to the lordship of Jesus Christ will discover authority in their submission, not the authority of an omniscient dictator or an invincible general, but the authority of the one who said, "I am meek and lowly in heart." Paul had at his disposal the authority of a miracle-working apostle, but he preferred to write to people in a problem-packed church, "By the meekness and gentleness of Christ, I appeal to you" (2 Cor. 10:1 NIV).

"Meekness" and "gentleness" are words not found in the vocabularies of most secular management experts today, or, for that matter, in the vocabularies of too many of God's servants; but they are found in the Bible. Moses was certainly the greatest leader in Hebrew history, yet he was "very meek, above all men who were on the face of the earth" (Num. 12:3). When Moses abandoned his meekness and lost his temper, he robbed God of glory and himself of a trip to the Holy Land. If he had looked upon those problem Jews as children instead of rebels (Num. 20:10), he would have saved himself a lot of trouble.

David was perhaps the number two leader in Hebrew history, and his confession was, "Your gentleness has made me great" (Ps. 18:35 NKJV). God stooped to David's plane and became, as it were, David's servant. "You stoop down to make me great" is the NIV translation, and it makes us think immediately of John 13:1–5 and Philippians 2:5–8. If the virtues of meekness and gentleness worked for Moses, David, Paul, and Jesus, they ought to work for us.

However, submission to Christ doesn't mean subservience to God's people. The statement "ourselves your servants *for Jesus' sake*" (2 Cor. 4:5, italics mine) defines the parameters: we serve God's people, not for our own sake or even for their sake, but "for Jesus' sake." We seek to do what Jesus would do, the way Jesus would do it, so that he alone gets the glory. Doing so isn't always easy, but it is necessary; it isn't always comfortable, but it is Christlike.

Authority is the privilege of exercising power, and it comes to us with the call of God and the confirmation of his people. When ministers are set apart for service by congregations that recognize God's call in their lives, those ministers have whatever authority goes with the calling. Ministers once were placed on pedestals and given special honor, but that day is long gone, which probably is a good thing. Today's pastor, instead of being an omniscient leader, is more of a playing coach who depends on teamwork more than on executive fiat.

Our second source of authority is the Word of God: "Thus saith the Lord." God's words to Ezekiel come to mind: "You shall speak my words to them, whether they hear or whether they refuse" (Ezek. 2:7 NKJV). This doesn't mean that God's authority stands behind all our ideas and interpretations, so our people need to know when we're sharing our own tentative opinions and when we're declaring God's truth. But the authority of the Scriptures must be the basis for what we do and say as the servants of God leading the people of God.

It's dangerous, however, to depend on professional and pulpit authority alone, which can easily lead to pseudoauthority or authoritarianism. Authority must be balanced by stature, what people see of the working of the Spirit in our own lives. Authority is given to us, but stature is something we must earn and comes with a price to pay. To be an example to the believer by obeying God's will and serving God's people is one of the highest honors possible in this life.

Yes, God's servant/leaders have authority, and they exercise it in love, balancing it with the stature they've gained by being faithful to the Lord and his people.

Why is it that God chose "servant leadership" as the pattern for his people to follow? There may be many reasons, but this much is certain: the servant/leader approach is the one that best glorifies God, encourages spiritual growth in the life of his servants, and meets the needs of God's people.

God is the glorious, eternal Servant/Leader. While it's true that all things serve him, it's also true that he serves all things. Jesus Christ is "sustaining all things by his powerful word" (Heb. 1:3 NIV). The word translated "sustaining" means that he is holding everything up so it doesn't fall down, he is holding it together so it doesn't fall apart, and he is carrying everything along to its determined conclusion. "In him all things hold together" (Col. 1:17 NIV). "For in him we live, and move, and have our being" (Acts 17:28 KJV). He has the whole world in his hands.

As the God of creation, he cares for his creatures, giving them what they need. "These all wait for you that you may give them their food is due season" (Ps. 104:27 NKJV). "You open your hand and satisfy the desire of every living thing" (Ps. 145:16 NKJV). He hears the cries of the hungry young ravens (Ps. 147:9), sees when the sparrow falls (Matt. 10:29), and knows every bird and beast in his creation (Ps. 50:11). God isn't a passive spectator in this vast universe. He's actively and compassionately in control.

When he ministered here on earth, Jesus certainly exemplified servant leadership. All kinds of people with all sorts of needs interrupted his schedule begging for help, and he graciously received them. As you read the four Gospels, you can't help but note the diversity of people who are found at Jesus' feet, from beggars to rulers, each of them with a special need, and Jesus met their needs.

The climax of his servant leadership on earth was at Calvary, where the Suffering Servant willingly sacrificed himself for the sins of the world. He arose from the dead and ascended to heaven, and from there he continues to serve his people as he intercedes for them (Heb. 7:25) and equips them for life and service (Heb. 13:20–21).

The Holy Spirit ministers to us so that we might minister to others. He fills us to make us channels, not reservoirs, so that we might share with others all that he gives us. The Spirit leads us and serves us so that we might become servants and leaders in his church, servant/leaders who glorify God because our lives are patterned after his.

Not only is servant leadership the way God works in his creation, but it's also the way he meets the needs of his people in their homes and churches. "Prone to wander," we need people to help lead us, and because of our many needs and burdens, we need people to minister to us and help to see us through.

The Christian husband and wife minister to each other and to their family by being dedicated servant/leaders in the home (Eph. 5:18–6:4). Their model is Jesus Christ ("even as Christ") and their motive is love. Growing up in that kind of an atmosphere, the children also learn to serve and to lead.

As members of the body of Christ and members of a local assembly, we become involved in serving and leading. We discover and develop our spiritual gifts and use them for the benefit of the whole church. No gift is unimportant and no member is insignificant. What we do, we do for Jesus' sake. "In Jesus," wrote Dietrich Bonhoeffer, "the service of God and the service of the least of the brethren were one."

But it's important to maintain balance as we minister to others. If all we do is lead, then we're giving good counsel from the Scriptures but we're not always meeting the immediate practical needs. "My little children, let us not love in word, neither in tongue; but in deed and in truth" (1 John 3:18 KJV). It's much easier to say "Go, I wish you well; keep warm and well fed" (James 2:16) than to sacrifice time and resources for which we may never be thanked.

However, if we meet the immediate material or physical needs but fail to share spiritual counsel, we're not really making a lasting investment in people's lives nor are we pointing them to Christ who alone meets the needs in the heart. We let our lights shine by serving others and doing good works, but our goal is to encourage people to glorify the Father in heaven (Matt. 5:16). By loving others, we let them know that God loves them far more than we do.

As servant/leaders, we meet the needs of different people at different times in different ways, and it's difficult to follow a policy or maintain consistency. Bernard of Clairvaux said, "Justice seeks out the merits of the case, but pity only regards the need." Jesus helped many people who never came back to thank him or even to trust him for salvation. In fact, one man he cured turned state's evidence against him (John 5:15–16)! But Jesus still went about doing good (Acts 10:38) because this was his purpose in coming and this glorified his Father.

Servant leadership is God's way of building his people spiritually. For one thing, it demands mature faith to believe that you win by surrendering, gain by losing, and lead by serving; but that's what Jesus promised. Most of us find it much easier to purchase the latest management best-seller and imitate the experts, or attend a "super seminar" where the gurus plagiarize the experts; but Jesus didn't take that approach. "The kings of the Gentiles lord it over them; and those who have authority over them are called 'Benefactors.' But not so with you, but let him who is the greatest among you become as the youngest, and the leader as the servant" (Luke 22:25–26 NASB).[2]

We abdicate neither our position nor our authority when we serve others. Instead, we prove that it's safe for the Lord and his people to give us that position and authority. "They must first be tested; and then if there is nothing against them, let them serve as deacons" (1 Tim. 3:10). What applies to deacons applies to any other leader: we must first prove that we know how to submit and serve, and then we can be trusted with authority. If we haven't learned how to submit to authority, how can we ever hope to exercise authority to the glory of God?

So, servant leadership helps build our faith. Submitted servants simply have to live by trusting God, depending on the Lord to work in them and through them to accomplish his will. "Behold, as the eyes of servants look to the hand of their masters, as the eyes of a maid to the hand of her mistress, so our eyes look to the LORD our God, until he has mercy on us" (Ps. 123:2 NKJV). "For we have no power against this great multitude that is coming against us; nor do we know what to do, but our eyes are upon You" (2 Chron. 20:12 NKJV).

Servant leadership also helps us grow in our love. Leaders don't really have to love. All they have to do is make plans and tell people what to do. This is how some ministers function. They don't weep with those who weep or seek to carry other people's burdens and manifest the love of Christ. But servants need love because servants are called upon to help difficult people with difficult problems. Being "important leaders," the priest and Levite can pass by on the other side and perhaps maintain a clear conscience; but the person with a servant's heart must go where the needy people are and pour the medicine of mercy.

Exclusive Christians, who consider themselves as the only ones with the truth, never really grow in their experience of God's love. According to Ephesians 3:18, we need "all the saints" to help us comprehend the greatness of God's love. That may include believers we disagree with. It's easy to practice "brotherly love" because brothers (and sisters) belong to the same family and share the same heritage. But Christian love doesn't mean we love because of likenesses; it means we love in spite of differences.

Jesus was a hands-on servant, touching lepers and corpses, beggars and the demon-possessed. He had to be hands-on in his ministry because his great love reached out to the helpless and drew them to himself. Christian love isn't so much how we feel, but whose needs we feel and whether or not we're willing to bear burdens that aren't ours "and so fulfill the law of Christ" (Gal. 6:2 KJV).

Servant leadership strengthens our faith and love, and faith and love manifest themselves in our lives in many ways, among them *patience*. Servants must be patient if their service is to be effective. Impatient servants might do more harm than good, as they put their own desires ("Let's get this over with!") ahead of the needs and feelings of those they're supposed to serve. Servants can't be double-minded and serve well; their whole focus must be on ministering to others and pleasing the Master. Hidden agendas are usually the evidence of hard hearts.

As servant/leaders, we sometimes cry out, "How long, O Lord, how long?" as we see the same people repeat the same mistakes and get into the same messes, and then ask us to help them out. We're tempted to look the other way, but then we remember our obligation to forgive even as we've been forgiven, even up to seventy times seven. Christian love simply means treating others the way the Lord treats us, and he's forgiven us the same sins many, many times.

Sincere servant/leaders find themselves growing in humility, which, as Andrew Murray reminds us, is not thinking meanly of ourselves but just not thinking of ourselves at all.[3] Humility is the soil in which the other Christian graces take root and bear fruit. It's that grace that when we know we have it, we lose it; but if we don't have it, we gain nothing else of spiritual value.

Jesus revealed his humility by becoming a servant and obeying the Father's will (Phil. 2:1–11). We learn humility by submitting as servants and doing the will of God from the heart (Eph. 6:6). The great leaders of Bible history began as servants—Moses and David as shepherds, Joshua as Moses' assistant, Joseph as a household servant, Elisha as Elijah's servant, and Timothy as Paul's attendant. If we want to hold a scepter, we must begin with a towel.

But that list of names—which could be expanded—reveals something else: true servant/rulers produce other servant/rulers because we all reproduce after our kind. Only in heaven will we see and understand the influence of the humble servant/leaders who have ministered since Christ first sent out his apostles to preach the gospel and heal the sick.

It's our privilege to be one of them—if we are willing to pay the price.

*T*here's a difference between exercising authority and being authoritarian, between commanding and demanding. Blessed are those leaders who know that Jesus Christ is Lord and they are second in command.

Chapter Six

The Purpose of Ministry Is the Glory of God

"Daddy, why is God's name hollow?"

Larry put down his book, as he always did when one of the children interrupted him, and took Danny on his lap.

"I didn't know God's name *was* hollow," he said. "Who told you that?"

"Every Sunday in church, that's how we pray—'Hollow be thy name.'"

Larry smiled and wondered what else his four-year-old son thought he heard at church. "No, Danny. The word isn't *hollow*, it's *hallowed*. To 'hallow' something means to make it very special, to honor it, to respect it. When we 'hallow' God's name, we show honor to the Lord and give him the glory he deserves."

Danny pondered his father's words and then said, "But 'hallow' is such a funny word."

Larry reached for his desk dictionary and opened to the entry *hallow*. "It comes from an old word that means 'holy,'" he explained, "so when we 'hallow' God's name, we treat it as holy and set it apart. You don't like it if the boys joke about your name, do you?"

Danny pursed his lips and frowned. "Billy calls me 'Daniel the spaniel' so I call him 'Billy goat.'"

Larry stifled a laugh and said, "Danny, we don't return evil for evil. It hurts you when Billy jokes about your name, and the Lord is grieved when we don't honor his name and set it apart as very special."

"You mean like when we dedicated the new Sunday school building?" asked Danny.

"That's a good comparison, son. We set the building apart to be used for God's glory. That's why there are some things we don't do in that building because it belongs especially to the Lord and his work."

"So when people swear they don't hallow God's name?"

"That's right, but we can rob God's name of glory in other ways besides swearing. If we take credit for what God does for us and don't praise him, that's robbing him of glory, and if we're more concerned about what *we* want than what he wants. If we don't thank God for his blessings but just take them for granted, we're not hallowing his name."

Danny kissed his father's cheek, jumped down from his lap, and ran to the back door, calling back, "Thanks, Dad! I'm going over to Billy's to play."

Larry didn't take up his book or his pen immediately but sat quietly, pondering the conversation. "Out of the mouths of babes," he said to himself. "What Danny said would make a good sermon topic: 'Are we *hollowing* God's name or *hallowing* it?' Who really gets the glory at First Church?"

He starting thinking of the times he was especially pleased with his preaching and was irritated because nobody complimented him. He recalled occasions when the special music was followed by applause instead of the holy hush that the song deserved. He winced when he remembered board meetings where, rather than glorifying God with good decisions, heated discussions had left the elders with bad feelings. And then there was the time he marched out of the finance committee meeting because he couldn't endure watching his precious budget being torn to shreds. He came back and apologized, but it took weeks for the hurts to heal.

Before long, Larry had forgotten his sermon preparation and was confessing his sins and praying, "Hallowed be thy name."

Doing the will of God from our hearts (Eph. 6:6) involves doing the right thing, in the right way, at the right time, and *for the right reason.* That reason, of course, is the glory of God.

An event recorded in Numbers 20:7–13 illustrates the point. Moses did a right thing (providing water) in a wrong way (smiting the rock instead of speaking to it) and for the wrong motive (to express his anger), and he paid dearly for his mistake. God gave his people water, but he deprived his servant of a trip to the Holy Land. Why? Because Moses didn't sanctify the Lord before his people and wasn't jealous for the glory of God.

It's a dangerous thing to take for ourselves the glory that belongs only to God. "I am the LORD; that is my name! I will not give my glory to another" (Isa. 42:8). That warning is so important that God repeated it in Isaiah 48:11. In the immediate context, the prophet is warning Israel against worshiping idols; but the warning is applicable to the church today. How easy it is to make idols out of our buildings, statistics, clever sermon outlines, and even our God-given abilities.

"No man can bear witness to Christ and to himself at the same time," wrote James Denney. "No man can give the impression that he himself is clever and that Christ is mighty to save."[1] That statement ought to be written in the front of every pastor's Bible and be hung on the wall of every pastor's study. During a crisis in his ministry, young G. Campbell Morgan faced the question, "Are you going to be a popular preacher or a faithful messenger of God?" Morgan's response was to burn his brilliant sermon outlines and recommit himself to be the messenger of the Lord, come what may.

One of the major themes of the Sermon on the Mount is *right motives for Christian living.* Do we pray, give, and practice spiritual disciplines in order to be praised by others, or to please the Lord and glorify him? Does it upset us when we aren't honored for the sacrifices we make and the work we do? Are we seeking to build our own kingdom or his kingdom? When people see our good works, do they praise us or glorify our Father in heaven?

Since God is the highest being in the universe, he is worthy of our worship and praise. In fact, the highest privilege we have as his children is to worship and serve him and do everything for his glory alone. God created the universe to glorify him (Num. 14:21; Ps. 19:1), so when we glorify the Lord, we cooperate with his creation and it cooperates with us. The great plan of salvation has as its goal "the praise of his glory" (Eph. 1:6, 12, 14), not just the rescuing of sinners from hell.

We can glorify God by the way we use our bodies (1 Cor. 6:19–20), which includes our willingness to serve and, if need be, to suffer and die for him (John 21:18–19; Phil. 1:19–22). We may not be called to be martyrs, but we can be "living sacrifices" that accomplish his will (Rom. 12:1–2). "This is to my Father's glory, that you bear much fruit, showing yourselves to be my disciples" (John 15:8).

Servants who are yielded to the Holy Spirit and filled with the Word of God will be guided to say and do those things that most honor the Lord (James 1:5). They will gradually develop a spiritual intuition that helps them make wise decisions, a God-given "radar" that warns them of trouble ahead. When our only desire is to glorify the Lord, we're more than willing to step aside and let others use their gifts. We don't care who gets the credit as long as God gets the glory.

If we aren't careful, the familiar phrase "the glory of God" can become a fuzzy cliché, a religious shield that we use to protect whatever "spiritual things" we may want to do. Charles Spurgeon said that he smoked cigars to the honor and glory of God, and perhaps he did, but Salvation Army leader Bramwell Booth called his words "a flippant and irreligious apology" that encouraged young men and women to use tobacco.[2] Yet God blessed both

Spurgeon and the Salvation Army in remarkable ways, which only proves that God can bless people we may disagree with.

In Scripture, "the glory of God" isn't so much a single attribute of God as the sum total of all that God is and does, which means that everything about God is glorious. He is glorious in power and holiness and therefore "triumphed gloriously" over the Egyptian army (Exod. 15:1, 6, 11). His work is glorious (Ps. 111:3), his name is glorious (Deut. 28:58), and so is his heavenly throne (Jer. 17:12). Whenever and wherever God reveals himself and his works, his glory is revealed.

The remarkable thing is that this glorious God has deigned to share his glory with his children! Jesus said, "I have given them the glory that you gave me" (John 17:22 NIV), and he prayed that his people might one day see his glory in heaven (John 17:24). God has called us to eternal glory (1 Peter 5:10), and the presence of the Holy Spirit in our lives is the assurance that we shall arrive in his glorious presence to share his glory forever (Eph. 1:13–14). In fact, according to Paul, we have already been glorified (Rom. 8:30), but the glory hasn't yet been fully revealed (Rom. 8:18–19).

Somebody has defined "glorifying God" as "making God look good before a godless world." The life and ministry of Jesus Christ are the best examples of this, for he manifested the glory of God in all he did and said. "And the Word became flesh and dwelt among us, and we beheld his glory" (John 1:14 NKJV). As he faced the cross, he was able to say with confidence to the Father, "I have glorified you on the earth. I have finished the work which you have given me to do" (John 17:4 NKJV). No servant of God could want to file a better work report!

God is glorified by turning weakness into power when we trust him, as when David defeated the giant Goliath (1 Sam. 17). Had David been a mature, experienced warrior, wearing strong armor and wielding fearsome weapons, the victory wouldn't have brought nearly as much glory to the Lord as when a teenager felled a giant with a stone hurled from a sling. *That has to be God!* "You come against me with sword and spear and javelin," David told Goliath, "but I come against you in the name of the LORD Almighty, the God of the armies of Israel, whom you have defied" (1 Sam. 17:45).

God is glorified when he transforms impossible situations into great victories, as when Jerusalem was surrounded by the Assyrian army in the days of King Hezekiah (Isa. 36–37). The king had no adequate resources for attacking Sennacherib's army, yet he and his people couldn't remain prisoners in Jerusalem. They wouldn't agree to Assyria's terms of peace, so they took the most logical way out and prayed to the Lord for help. He answered in a way that honored his name because only he could have done it. Hezekiah and his people woke up one morning to discover 185,000 enemy soldiers dead on the battlefield, *and this had to be the work of God.*

Christians in tight places who experience God's help will bring glory to him, whether it's Joseph in prison, Moses in Egypt, David in the wilderness of Judea, Esther in the Persian court, Peter in prison, or Paul on a sinking ship. When God permits special trials to come to us, our families, or our churches, one of his purposes is to give us opportunity to glorify his name. "However, if you suffer as a Christian, do not be ashamed, but praise God that you bear that name" (1 Peter 4:16).

For the most part, the people we serve in our congregations don't look like Josephs, Esthers, or Davids, nor do we; but the same God who glorified himself in the lives of "ordinary people" in ancient days will glorify himself in our lives today if we will trust him. The patient paraplegic in the wheelchair may not get as much publicity as David, but God is glorified in that life just the same. The uncomplaining retired couple that lives frugally so they can support a missionary is glorifying God by depending on his grace and provision. When people see us and wonder how we keep going with joy and endurance, they know *it has to be God.* As Dr. Bob Cook was wont to say, "If you can explain what's going on, God didn't do it."

The Christian ministry brings with it many subtle temptations to pride and selfish ambition, and these must be resisted to the very end. God will not share his glory with another.

While pastors today don't have the vocational stature they once held, they are still looked upon as people of authority. They stand before congregations week after week, declaring the message of God. Behind the sermon (we trust) is the authority of the Word of God. Pastors can use their spiritual authority to build up the people, or they can use the people to build up their authority. They can be either shepherds that *lead* the sheep or hirelings that *drive* the sheep and open the way for a march of ministerial triumph.

The pastor is also a sympathetic counselor, and this ministry can be fraught with peril. He comes to people during seasons of both joy and sorrow and enters little by little into their personal lives, hearing privileged communications and sharing hidden hurts. What he knows can be used as tools to build with or weapons to fight with. It all depends on his motives. Weak people can become emotionally dependent on him, and the ambitious pastor can feed his ego by catering to them. Of such ingredients ministerial indiscretions and secret sins are born, usually leading to ministerial tragedies.

Of course, the faithful and insightful minister will conquer these temptations and use these experiences to the glory of God. He will detect when a personal relationship is becoming a trap instead of a bridge, or when a problem person is seeking consoling rather than counseling. He will be honest with himself and deal decisively with his emotions, remembering our Lord's warning about cutting off the hand or gouging out the eye. Strong words, yes, but surgery is better than tragedy.

Whether we realize it or not, we communicate to our people the attitudes we have toward them and the work of the ministry, and it doesn't take God's people long to size up their shepherd. Do they see in us the joy and challenge of Christian service, or the drudgery and dullness of doing a job we don't want to do for people we really don't like? If we aren't careful, we can become elder brothers who work dutifully but don't enjoy it, who think highly of ourselves but criticize the brethren, and who have a hidden agenda that makes us disagree with the Father's will. We become outsiders looking in, but not partaking of the joyful feast.

As he focuses on the glory of God, the devoted minister will avoid becoming an idol to himself or to his people. If the pastor doesn't sincerely seek to glorify God, the church may end up glorifying the pastor; then both the minister and the church will be in trouble. We must beware of living on compliments lest we find ourselves confusing God's will with Satan's plans (Matt. 16:21–23). It has well been said that a leader suffers more from his disciples than from his critics, and this is especially true in Christian ministry.

Fame and popularity aren't the same as success. When God decides to magnify a servant's name, that's one thing. When we start promoting ourselves, however, that's quite something else. God told Joshua, "Today I will begin to exalt you in the eyes of all Israel" (Josh. 3:7); and by magnifying his servant, the Lord glorified himself and accomplished great things. But Joshua's experience was a far cry from the apostles' debate over which of them was the greatest! Only God is great.

God's servants are in special danger when their names are widely known and their works are praised. It was written of Uzziah, one of Judah's most famous kings, "His fame spread far and wide, for he was greatly helped until he became powerful" (2 Chron. 26:15). Uzziah forgot the first lesson of Leadership 101, "For when I am weak, then I am strong" (2 Cor. 12:10).

God has ways of keeping his servants weak so they'll get their strength from him alone. Rarely do their congregations know the pain that pastors feel, the burdens they bear, and the battles they wage in private; but the Lord knows and supplies the needed grace. When the Father puts his children into the furnace of affliction, he keeps his eye on the clock and his hand on the thermostat. He knows how much and how long. Our task is to trust him and pray that we will come forth like gold (Job 23:10).

In his excellent *Lectures on Preaching,* Phillips Brooks advised: "Never allow yourself to feel equal to your work. If you ever find that spirit growing on you, be afraid, and instantly attack your hardest piece of work, try to convert your toughest infidel, try to preach on your most exacting theme, to show yourself how unequal to it all you are."[3] Brooks might have added: And consider that your calling is to glorify God. If that doesn't humble us, nothing will.

At a denominational conference, a musical group sang a contemporary song in a most exciting "show-biz" manner and evoked loud cheers and applause. People were smiling and saying, "Aren't they good? Wasn't their choreography entertaining?" The group was followed by a pastor with multiple sclerosis who from his wheelchair sang "No One Ever Cared for Me Like Jesus." When he was finished, a holy hush moved over the congregation. There were tears in people's eyes, and they were thinking, "Isn't our God wonderful? Oh, how we ought to love him more!" No cheers and applause, just worship.

When ministry becomes performance, then the sanctuary becomes a theater, the congregation becomes an audience, worship becomes entertainment, and man's applause and approval become the measure of success. But when ministry is for the glory of God, his presence moves into the sanctuary. Even the unsaved visitor will fall down on his face, worship God, and confess that God is among us (1 Cor. 14:25).

The words of James Denney are worth reading again: "No man can bear witness to Christ and to himself at the same time. No man can give the impression that he himself is clever and that Christ is mighty to save."

The purpose of ministry is the glory of God.

---

*T*here is nothing God cannot do for a faithful servant who thinks only of the glory of God.

Chapter Seven

The Tools of Ministry Are the Word of God and Prayer

hanksgiving Day was always a special time for the Jarvis family. Their sons and daughters-in-law made a point of being "back home again in Indiana," bringing seven excited grandchildren with them. The gathering of the clan was a family tradition that everybody hoped would continue uninterrupted until the return of the Lord.

Dad and Mom Jarvis had retired after pastoring three churches for a total of forty-three years, and they were pleased that their two boys had followed in their footsteps.

"Well, son, how goes the battle?" Dad asked Daniel while the men cleared the table for coffee and pie. Dan was now in his third year of ministry and wasn't having an easy time.

Dan hesitated, not wanting to cast gloom over the festive occasion. "Well, Dad, the battle's going on and, believe me, it's really a battle."

"The third year's the hardest because the honeymoon's over," his father commented. "The fifth year is often when things start to open up, but the tenth is the toughest. If you hang in there until number ten, that's when the church turns the corner."

"The way things are going, Dad, I may not last for five years. I may end up standing on that corner all alone."

"Sure you'll make it!" his father exclaimed. "The Lord's on your side and you can't lose!"

Dan wasn't so sure it was that easy. Furthermore, he didn't have the people skills and the staying power that helped make his father such a successful shepherd. If Dan had his choice, he'd rather be coaching in a Bible college or running a Christian camp.

"Seriously, Dad, what really builds a church? No clichés, now!" he asked.

"Two resources, son: the Word of God and prayer. According to Acts 6:4, the apostles devoted themselves to prayer and the ministry of the Word. That's the example you want to follow."

Dan's older brother Joe spoke up from across the table. "Believe me, Dan, I know from experience that Dad's right. During my first three years at First Church, I tried every gimmick I could find to get things moving, and they all bombed."

Joe's wife interrupted. "Tell him what your priorities were then," she said in a teasing voice.

With an embarrassed smile, Joe continued. "Okay, Laurie, but now we can both laugh about it. I thought I should be an administrator, running programs and making five-year plans. Counseling was another priority, and I spent a lot of time listening to people's problems and acting omniscient. Sunday mornings weren't about worship. It was mainly entertainment. I confess I didn't do much Bible study, and I prayed only when I was in deep trouble. Then I followed Dad's counsel and got serious about preaching and teaching the Word and praying for and with my people. It took time, and we lost some people, but then good things began to happen—and they're still happening."

Dad Jarvis spoke up. "You've got to keep things balanced, boys. If all you have in the church is prayer and no Bible, you end up with lots of heat but no light, zeal without knowledge. But plenty of Bible without prayer gives you light without heat. You don't have a church; you have a Bible school. Bible knowledge without prayer has a way of puffing people up. It takes both the Word of God and prayer to make balanced Christians and to build a balanced church. This approach may not be popular, but it's biblical—and it works."

During the three-hour drive home the next day, Dan pondered what his father and brother had said. He had to confess that they were right. But focusing on prayer and the Word of God would mean making some radical changes in his own lifestyle and in the program of the church. It wasn't going to be easy.

The first crisis the apostolic church faced and successfully weathered is recorded in Acts 6:1–7, the disagreement between the Hebrews and the Hellenists over the neglect of their widows in the daily distribution of food. However, the problem involved much more than feeding people, as important as that is, for it was basically a struggle between *church ministry* and *church structure.* After all, a growing church, like a growing child, occasionally requires new "clothes," and the early church was willing to modify its structure to keep organization from obstructing the progress of the ministry.

But what caused the problem? Was it just a matter of geography and prejudice, with the Hebrew-speaking Jews resenting the Greek-speaking Jews who came from outside the Holy Land? Not at all. According to the biblical record, the problem was caused by *the apostles,* the spiritual leaders of the church! (Bottlenecks are usually at the top.) The apostles were so busy serving tables that they were neglecting prayer and the ministry of the Word, and this created a spiritual deficiency in the body that led to disagreement and division.

In short, the apostles' spiritual priorities were confused, and it showed up in their ministries. Once the deacons were appointed and began to serve, the problem was solved.

The Scottish novelist George MacDonald said it best: "In whatever man does without God, he must fail miserably—or succeed more miserably." The busier we are, the easier it is to leave God out of our work even though we know that Jesus said "apart from me you can do nothing" (John 15:5 NIV). The church that ignores the Word of God and prayer is living on substitutes, or perhaps we should say *dying* on substitutes, no matter how alive the church body appears to be.

Devotion to the Word of God and prayer will give balance to our lives and to our ministries. This is proved by some of the leading servants of God found in Scripture. Moses met God on the mount and interceded for Israel, then came down and taught them the Word that God had given him (Exod. 32–34). The prophet Samuel told Israel and their new king, "Moreover, as for me, far be it from me that I should sin against the LORD in ceasing to pray for you: but I will teach you the good and the right way" (1 Sam. 12:23 NKJV). Both Moses and Samuel depended on the Word of God and prayer.

Daniel studied the Scriptures and learned God's plan for the Jewish nation, and then he turned to prayer and asked God to forgive his people and work on their behalf (Dan. 9). In his epistles, Paul taught his readers doctrine and then paused to pray for them. The Epistle to the Ephesians is a good example of this kind of balanced ministry. Paul even prayed for believers he had never met who would be reading his letters (Col. 2:1–2).

Jesus promised, "If you abide in me, and my words abide in you [*that's the Word of God*], you will ask what you desire [*that's prayer*], and it shall be done for you" (John 15:7 NKJV). Our Lord practiced what he preached by spending the early hours of the day in prayer and then going from place to place teaching the Word (Mark 1:35–39).

The Holy Spirit has chosen to work in our lives and in his church by means of the Word of God and prayer, and for us to substitute anything else means disobeying God, grieving the Spirit, and missing the blessings God has for his people. In the early church, the Word of God and prayer gave the believers the wisdom they needed for making decisions and choosing leaders (Acts 1); and remember, they had only the Old Testament to consult. We're privileged today to have a complete Bible.

Peter's sermon at Pentecost was a declaration of God's Word, and it was preceded by ten days of concerted prayer, so it's no wonder that thousands were converted to Christ (Acts 2). When the church was attacked by its enemies, the believers prayed to God for help and leaned heavily on the Word of God (Acts 4:23–30), which kept them from giving up. It's worth noting that Paul combines the Word of God and prayer when he describes the Christian's armor (Eph. 6:17–18), for it takes both if we're to defeat the enemy.[1]

It was while the church leaders in Antioch were ministering the Word and praying that God called Paul and Barnabas to take the gospel message to the Gentiles (Acts 13), and this has always been the biblical way to find laborers (Luke 10:1–2). That's why Paul blessed the Ephesian elders as he did when he met with them at Miletus: "And now, brethren, I commend you to God [*prayer*], and to the word of his grace [*the Word*], which is able to build you up, and to give you an inheritance among all them who are sanctified" (Acts 20:32 KJV).

So, like two wings carrying a bird in flight or two oars propelling a boat through the water, the Word of God and prayer keep us balanced and moving ahead. Because all of us have our likes and dislikes, our strengths and weaknesses, we're prone to emphasize what we enjoy most and do best. Unfortunately, this produces an unbalanced ministry and eventually an unbalanced church. The studious minister locks himself in his study and pores over his books, while his outgoing activist brother across town prays earnestly for God's help as he visits prospects, shepherds his needy flock, and seeks to win the lost. Ideally, both men should be involved in both pursuits, but it doesn't always happen that way. Balance is something we must constantly work at, but the Holy Spirit is perfectly balanced in his character and ministry, and enables us to keep the spiritual equilibrium we need, which is also demanded by a growing church.

As we study the Scriptures, we learn what God is like, what God wants done, and how God wants to help us do it. We discover our spiritual riches in Christ and the resources available to his church. However, to revel in theology but not put it into practice is to be guilty of faith without works. On the other hand, to seek to obey the Word without praying for God's help is to be guilty of arrogance, for without Christ, we can do nothing. Prayerlessness doesn't simply make us weak or handicapped so that our ministry is difficult. Lack of prayer paralyzes us so that we're not able to do anything that will produce lasting fruit to the glory of God.

The better we understand God's Word, the better we're able to pray; the more we pray, the more the Holy Spirit can teach us from the Word and help us obey it. According to Romans 10:17, our faith should grow as we increase our understanding of the Scriptures, and according to John 7:17, the more we obey God's Word by faith, the better we'll understand his truth. Studying the Word for truth and praying to God for blessing on service are not competitive activities; they're the best of friends.

Because the Word of God is living and powerful, wonderful things can happen when we share it with others, whether we minister as preachers, teachers, counselors, or witnesses. "Thy commandment is exceedingly broad" (Ps. 119:96 NASB) and can meet the many needs of all kinds of people.

When we share the Word, it's like bringing light in the darkness (Ps. 119:130; 2 Cor. 4:6), planting seed (Luke 8:11), cleansing with pure water (John 15:3; Eph. 5:26), dispensing healing medicine (Ps. 107:20), serving nourishing food (Matt. 4:4; 1 Cor. 3:1–3; 1 Peter 2:2), wielding a powerful sword (Eph. 6:17; Heb. 4:12), and investing spiritual wealth (2 Tim. 2:2). According to Psalm 119, God's Word can give guidance to the perplexed (v. 105), victory to the tempted (v. 11), joy to the discouraged (vv. 14, 111, 162), encouragement to the hopeless (v. 49), peace to the troubled (v. 165), freedom to the bound (vv. 45, 133), new life to the defeated (vv. 25, 37, 40, 88), and much more.

Our speaking words into the air may seem like a futile activity because the sounds vanish so quickly, but God's promise is, "I am watching to see that my word is fulfilled" (Jer. 1:12). No word of God is ever lost or fails to fulfill its divine purpose. "So is my word that goes out from my mouth: it will not return to me empty, but will accomplish what I desire, and achieve the purpose for which I sent it" (Isa. 55:11).

The apostles knew what worked and what God could bless and use. That's why they said, "But we will give ourselves continually to prayer, and to the ministry of the word" (Acts 6:4 NKJV).

That needs to be our affirmation of faith as well.

The most important part of your life is the part that only God sees, so let's start with your personal devotional time with the Lord—that daily discipline of meditation, examination, and intercession that is absolutely essential to Christian service.

More than one Christian worker has confessed the absence of a disciplined and satisfying devotional life, in spite of the fact that the Scriptures command it and the lives of God's esteemed servants commend it. "The commentators are good instructors," Charles Spurgeon told his pastoral students, "but the Author Himself is far better, and prayer makes a direct appeal to Him and enlists Him in our cause."[2]

"But I work on sermons and lessons all week long," some ministers protest, "and I certainly spend plenty of time in the Bible! Isn't that enough of a good thing?"

But preparing meals for other people doesn't guarantee that the chef is feeding himself. Likewise if you aren't allowing the Lord to feed you the nourishing Word of God, how can you ever serve him adequately? Like Jeremiah (15:16), Ezekiel (2:9–3:4), and John (Rev. 10:8–11), we must pause in our prophesying to eat the Word of God that he hands us. That's what keeps us going.

The pastor comes to his scheduled devotional time, not as a preacher looking for ideas to share with others, but as a common sinner needing God's grace for himself, a submissive servant listening for God's will, a hungry worshiper seeking God's face. In the holy of holies, all of us are amateurs and there's no room for professionals. God isn't impressed with our credentials. If during our meditating, the Spirit does give us an idea for a sermon, we should quickly jot it down and then immediately return to communing with God because that's why we're there.

If we read Scripture systematically, with a mind open to learn and a will ready to obey, it's remarkable how each day the Spirit of God gives us just the truth we need. The servant who looks humbly to the Master's hand (Ps. 123) and waits early at the Master's door (Prov. 8:34) will never be disappointed. Can we plead for bread and expect to receive a stone?

Certainly the Spirit must guide us in our praying (Rom. 8:26–27), but it's also good to have a list of the prayer needs that burden us the most—people who need to be saved, problems that must be solved, provisions for the work of the Lord around the world. More than one servant has found a prayer journal to be helpful for keeping track of requests and God's answers. However you do it, be sure all things are done "decently and in order."

But true prayer involves battles as well as blessings. Like Epaphras, we ought to be "laboring fervently in prayer" for our people (Col. 4:12). The enemy is strong and his strategy is subtle, so God's warriors need to put on the whole armor of God daily and trust the Lord for victory (Eph. 6:10–18). "Warfare praying" attacks Satan's strongholds (2 Cor. 10:1–6) and claims the power of God to defeat the enemy.[3] The old hymn that admonishes us to "put on the gospel armor, each piece put on with prayer" has focused on an important part of prayer, the part that the enemy wishes we wouldn't practice.

But it isn't enough simply to start the day with worship, meditation, and prayer. We must maintain that spiritual posture throughout the day and "abide under the shadow of the Almighty" (Ps. 91:1). The Old Testament priest who burned the incense on the golden altar—a picture of prayer (Ps. 141:2)—carried the fragrance with him all day, and so should we. Like Nehemiah, we must "keep the receiver off the hook" and send frequent messages to the Lord as we labor with the people in building the wall.[4]

Cultivating a satisfying devotional life isn't easy for any Christian, especially the servants of God who handle spiritual things day after day. The late Vance Havner wrote, "The devil is in constant conspiracy against a preacher who really prays, for it has been said that what a minister is in his prayer closet is what he is, no more, no less." It's obvious that no Christian can rise any higher than his or her prayer life, and only the heavenly Father knows what we're doing when we should be praying.

Important as they are, the preacher's prayers alone can't get the job done. He must have behind him the power of a praying church. When a visitor asked Spurgeon the secret of his fruitful ministry, he thought for a moment and then replied, "My people pray for me." What more could a minister want?

It isn't important *when* the church prays, but it is important *that* the church prays, for great power is released when God's people join together to cry out to the Lord. For centuries, the weekly church prayer meeting was called the "powerhouse of the church." However, times are changing and weeknight meetings devoted primarily to prayer seem to be a thing of the past. There are exceptions, of course, and we're grateful for them, but the decline of the weeknight prayer service seems to be the result of a general malady in the land.

We are losing something, but we need not despair. The decline of one prayer service need not signal the end of prayer in the church. A praying pastor will always build a praying church. If he can't gather the saints once a week for an evening of public prayer, he'll see to it that his people are praying from house to house and in special groups. Surely he'll meet regularly with his church leaders, not to drink coffee and discuss business, but to beseech the throne of grace for the blessings sorely needed. He'll see to it that various groups within the church organization engage in systematic prayer whenever they meet and also on special occasions. Each Lord's Day, he'll want some of the people to join him in prayer for the ministry of the day and ask God to give him power for proclaiming the Word. Like Paul, the praying pastor will not be ashamed to ask the saints for the prayer support he so desperately needs.

Our people need to know not only what the prayer burdens are, but also how the Lord has answered, since both are encouragements to prayer. Some churches appoint a "prayer secretary" who handles all this information and makes sure the church family is kept informed. Thanks to the telephone, fax machines, and E-mail, it isn't at all difficult to let people know what God is doing as a result of his people praying. The telephone "prayer chain" is the heartbeat of many local churches and ought to be encouraged.

But back to the pastor.

The old divines used to pray in their studies as they prepared the sermon, but they also prayed for help before they delivered the sermon and often while they were preaching. Saintly Robert Murray M'Cheyne even wrote ejaculatory prayers like "Master, help!" at the end of his sermon outlines, and while he was preaching, his heart was crying out to God for power. "You preached today as though you came from the throne of heaven," a church officer said to Alexander Whyte one Lord's Day. Whyte quietly replied, "Maybe I did."

But these men of old also retired *after they had preached* and watered the sown seed with their prayers and tears. "We are tempted to pray *before preaching*," Alexander Whyte wrote to a friend about to be ordained, "because we are afraid at the people and at our work; but prayer for ourselves and the people *after* preaching is much neglected."[5] Congregations in Canada and Great Britain have the blessed practice of sitting down after the benediction and quietly meditating and praying before leaving the sanctuary. In the United States, however, ministers and worshipers are prone to engage in immediate convivial fellowship after a service. While it's important to meet people, it's also important to get alone with God in prayer and seek his special blessing on the Word.

Now, of the things which we have spoken, this is the sum: the church is a divine institution that cannot succeed without divine power, and that power comes through prayer and the ministry of the Word of God. Methods and approaches change from decade to decade, but the essentials remain: "[We] will give our attention to prayer and the ministry of the word" (Acts 6:4 NIV). Or, as Eugene Peterson paraphrases it in *The Message,* "Meanwhile, we'll stick to our assigned tasks of prayer and speaking God's Word."

We start with our own example, for God knows that we can't exhort others to do what we aren't doing ourselves. Once our own devotional life is healthy, then we can start encouraging people to pray individually, in their family devotions, and in the various groups that make up the church family. We organize a system for receiving and transmitting prayer requests and answers to prayer, and through it all, we're careful to give God the glory.

For he has ordained that his house shall be called a house of prayer for all nations (Mark 11:17).

*W*ithout the Word of God and prayer, ministry is nothing but religious activity. Learn everything you can that will help you better serve God's people, but be sure to saturate your ministry with the Word of God and prayer.

Chapter Eight

The Privilege of Ministry Is Growth

It didn't take Don and Lori long to discover that Mom and Pop Sewell had big hearts, open ears, and closed lips. Their home was a refuge for this young pastor and his wife and the Sewell door was always open to them.

"I hope the saints aren't giving you too much trouble," Pop said as he poured the coffee. "We're a rowdy bunch, so don't pay any attention to our griping. Just do what the Lord wants you to do and it'll all turn out fine."

Don smiled. "Oh, the congregation's been great to us—well, except for a couple of people. But that's not my biggest problem."

Mom Sewell handed Don a piece of homemade apple pie and asked, "Let me guess what your biggest problem is."

"Go ahead."

"Your biggest problem is yourself," she said quietly. "You really don't think you've got what it takes to pastor the church."

Don hurriedly took a bite of the pie so he wouldn't have to answer. However, Lori answered for him.

"You're right, Mom Sewell. It takes all the praying and encouraging the Lord gives me to keep Don going. We've been here only two years, and he's written his resignation five times."

Pop Sewell smiled and poured himself another cup of coffee. "Well, we're sure glad you didn't read any of them to the church," he said, "because it would have done you and us a lot of damage, but mostly you."

Don squirmed in his chair. "I just don't think I've got what it takes, that's all. Is there anything wrong with being honest?"

"Not as long as you're honest about the right things," Pop Sewell replied. "The thing to be honest about is the simple fact that *nobody* has what it takes to serve the Lord. That's what makes serving him so wonderful. It gives you a glorious opportunity to grow."

Don frowned. "Then I'll be your pastor forever, because I've sure got a lot of growing to do!"

Pop grinned and turned to his wife. "Mother, tell these young people what you went through the first year we were starting rural Sunday schools in Arkansas."

"Well, you won't believe this," she said, wiping her lips with her napkin, "but Dad was ready to give up the ministry every Monday morning. He didn't write any official resignations, you understand, but if the regional superintendent had shown up on our doorstep any given Monday, Dad would have told him, 'I quit!'"

Dad Sewell laughed. "Pastor Don, I had the same problem then that you have now. I was looking at my weaknesses and failings instead of looking to the Lord for his sufficiency. Remember, son, it was the great apostle Paul who asked, 'And who is sufficient for these things?' Then he answered his own question: 'But our sufficiency is of God.'[1] You see, ministry makes the man as much as the man makes the ministry. No challenge, no growth. If you run away, you'll just face the same things in the next place, so why not do your growing here where people love you?"

Don finally spoke up. "I remember a chapel message at seminary and the speaker told us that the reward for faithful work is more work. I thought he was crazy, but now I see that he was dead right. I either grow or go, *and I don't want to go.*"

As Don backed the car out of the driveway, he asked his wife, "Lori, what did Mom Sewell hand you at the door?"

"I'll show it to you when we get home."

No sooner was the car in their garage when Lori took a small picture frame out of her purse. In it was a Bible verse, written in Mom Sewell's copperplate script. Lori handed it to Don and said, "This is for both of us." It read: "Should such a man as I flee?" (Neh. 6:11 NKJV).

Don squeezed her hand. "I think it's time to grow."

The best thing about being a winning athlete isn't so much the publicity or the financial reward. The best thing is just being the kind of person in mind and body who can compete with confidence, whether you win or lose. Long after the applause has ended and the money has been spent, the successful athlete still has a healthy body, a zest for competition, and an excitement about achievement that keeps life interesting.

So it is with the Christian ministry. The reward of ministry isn't appreciation from the congregation, as welcome as that is, or even the numerical growth of the congregation. The real reward is the spiritual growth that makes us better servants, able to lay hold of the challenges God sends our way. That's why Paul cautioned Timothy, "Take pains with these things; be absorbed in them, so that your progress may be evident to all" (1 Tim. 4:15 NASB).

The word translated "progress" means "pioneer advance into new territory." Not everybody enjoys being a pioneer; some of us feel more comfortable as settlers. But God doesn't call his servants to rest on their laurels and stop moving. He manages to shake things up occasionally so that we have to grow and trust him to make us sufficient for the task. "If you have run with footmen and they have tired you out," God asked grumbling Jeremiah, "then how can you compete with horses? If you fall down in a land of peace, how will you do in the thicket of the Jordan?" (Jer. 12:5 NASB).

The pictures of ministry that Paul painted in 2 Timothy 2 all suggest that God has called us to expend energy and effort, for you can't be a successful steward (v. 2), soldier (vv. 3–4), athlete (v. 5), or farmer (v. 6) and sit around doing nothing. As stewards, we have spiritual wealth to protect and invest; as soldiers, we have a war to wage and an enemy to defeat; as athletes, we have a race to run; and as farmers, we have soil to plow and seed to sow. And while we're doing all these things and more, we have the glorious opportunity to grow and become more like Jesus Christ.

What Paul wrote about Christian giving can be applied to Christians who give of themselves in ministry:

> But this I say: He who sows sparingly will also reap sparingly, and he who sows bountifully will also reap bountifully. . . . And God is able to make all grace abound toward you, that you, always having all sufficiency in all things, have an abundance for every good work. . . . Now may he who supplies seed to the sower, and bread for food, supply and multiply the seed you have sown and increase the fruits of your righteousness, *while you are enriched in everything.* . . .
>
> (2 Cor. 9:6, 8, 10–11 NKJV; italics mine)

God's ministers aren't manufacturers; they're distributors. As God supplies the spiritual seed and bread to us, we gladly share it with others, and we ourselves are enriched in the process. Remember, Jesus compared the will of God and the work of God to food that nourishes us (John 4:34), and where there's nourishment, there will be development.

The privilege of ministry is growth, but the tragedy of ministry is arrested development and stagnation. It's easy to reach a comfortable plateau, settle down to enjoy the scenery, and forget that standing still in the Christian life really means gradually slipping backward. When we stop growing, ministry becomes stagnant, even boring, and what we do becomes safe and predictable. Why rock the boat when it's so enjoyable to drift?

Arrested development produces painful consequences in the life of the servant of God. To begin with, he starts living on past experiences and has nothing fresh from the Lord to share with his people. The bread is stale and moldy and the seed doesn't germinate. The family that lives on leftovers may survive, but it won't be too healthy or happy.

The minister also becomes protective and defensive. He's afraid of new people because they might bring with them dangerous new ideas, and he depends on his "fan club" in the church to protect him. He isn't able to face honest criticism, so the people who want something better either leave the church or become the silent opposition. The congregation attracts people who resist change and it repels newcomers who might introduce relevance and excitement.

"There's no friction in our church," the pastor proudly announces, while the more discerning saints say to themselves, "Yes, no friction because there's no motion." Few places are as quiet as a cemetery.

Convinced that they know all they need to know in order to do all they have to do, stagnant servants are blind to their own needs and the needs of their people. They need to pray that ancient anonymous prayer:

> From the cowardice that shrinks from new truth,
> From the laziness that is content with half-truths,
> From the arrogance that thinks it knows all truth,
> O God of truth, deliver us!

The absence of problems in a church usually signals that people aren't being challenged, organizations are becoming ossified, and the enemy is satisfied. Vital, vibrant Christianity has been replaced by polite piety, church officers are busy running the machinery, and the preacher is content to have it so. But if you listen closely, you can hear the sad voice of the grieved Holy Spirit saying, "I know your works, that you have a name that you are alive, but you are dead" (Rev. 3:1 NKJV). Campbell Morgan called it "reputation without reality," and it has ruined many a ministry.

How does the servant of God keep growing, no matter how many years of ministry he has experienced?

First, *he seeks always to be himself.* Nothing robs us of maturity like trying to be what we aren't or imitating somebody we'd rather be. Immature ministers often have what A. W. Tozer called "the fan-club mentality" and try to be like whatever famous preacher captures their imagination. On all occasions, be yourself—your best self—and trust God to use you. Don't waste time and energy being an imitation. Let God make you into an original.

Second, he *keeps his life open to God and His truth.* Arthur F. Holmes reminds us that "all truth is God's truth," so the opportunities for learning and growing are infinite and no doubt will continue when we're in eternity. People who grow read widely and aren't afraid to read authors they disagree with, for maturing people realize that in this life "we know in part" (1 Cor. 13:9). When it comes to understanding God's truth, nobody has a corner on the market.

So, what should we do? How about tackling a tough book and working your way through it as though you had to pass an exam? That means taking notes, thinking about what's written, and examining your own ideas in the light of what the book says. Your choice may be a classic you've always wanted to read, or perhaps a new book on theology or some other aspect of ministry. Just be sure it's a book with meat and bones so your mental muscles will have something nutritious to chew on. Read a theologian whose views are different from yours, or a biography of somebody outside your usual sphere of interest. A book that doesn't challenge us isn't likely to change us, so be courageous in your selections.

Third, *he is honest with God in his devotional life.* It's bad enough for the stagnant servant to lie to others, but when he starts lying to God in his praying and meditating, he's really in trouble. We must accept what God says in his Word, apply it first to ourselves, and then talk honestly to God about what he wants us to do. Openness and honesty with God in the secret place will deliver us from deception and evasion in the marketplace.

Honesty with God ought to result in honesty with ourselves, and that means measuring ourselves accurately. Do we know what areas of life and ministry need to be strengthened? Are we willing to turn to others for help and admit that we need it? Can we make plans for actions that will improve our skills and then stick with those plans?

Fourth, *he is accountable to others and learns from them.* Jesus sent his apostles out two by two because God's servants need each other. "Two are better than one," advised Solomon, "because they have a good reward for their labor. For if they fall, one will lift up his companion. But woe to him who is alone when he falls, for he has no one to help him up" (Eccl. 4:9–10 NKJV). This doesn't leave much room for the "Lone Ranger" type of servant who commands everybody but answers to nobody.

What Thomas Merton wrote about men in monastic orders can be applied to every professed Christian.

> The most dangerous man in the world is the contemplative who is guided by nobody. He trusts his own visions. He obeys the attractions of an interior voice but will not listen to other men. He identifies the will of God with anything that makes him feel, within his own heart, a big, warm, sweet interior glow. The sweeter and the warmer the feeling is the more he is, convinced of his own infallibility. . . . [S]uch a man can wreck a whole city or a religious order or even a nation. The world is covered with scars that have been left in its flesh by visionaries like these.[2]

"As iron sharpens iron," wrote Solomon, "so a man sharpens the countenance of his friend" (Prov. 27:17 NKJV).

The growing minister, therefore, cultivates a network of people (not all of them Christian workers or even believers) who stimulate his thinking, challenge his ideas, stretch his mental and spiritual muscles, and occasionally shoot down his pet dreams and plans. Apostles and prophets received their enlightenment directly from God, but we today can't boast of that luxury. We read God's Word, pray, meditate, talk things over with friends, and then make our decisions, always checking our motives and trusting the Lord to give us the guidance we need.

Fifth, *he determines to send his roots down deep and stay as long as the Lord directs.* While not everybody is supposed to invest a lifetime in one place, it's certain that more ministers could stay longer if they'd cultivate their roots and grow. Of course, this means bracing for the storm, digging in for the long haul, and standing firm in the faith no matter what problems the church might face.

The difficult situations of ministry encourage growth and reveal that a maturing process is going on. It has well been said that a crisis doesn't make the man but reveals what the man is made of. "Whatever is formed for long duration arrives slowly to its maturity," said Samuel Johnson, a statement I sometimes recall when our church congregation sings "Take Time to Be Holy."

We can't make the most of our privilege of growing if our commitments are tentative, our relationships shallow, and our vision limited. Granted, sometimes the congregation doesn't make it easy for the pastor to remain long on the field. Unfortunately, some churches have the reputation of chewing up their ministers and spitting them out. No matter what the pastor does, it isn't right, and the "power people" in the congregation see to it that three years is the average length of stay. If the pastor stays longer, he might start uncovering the real problems and offering some dangerous solutions.

But the Lord can help us weather the storms in the valley and patiently guide the flock into greener pastures and quieter waters. It takes time, so we plan to stay. It takes faith, so we rest on the promises of God. It takes courage, so we pray. And it takes love, so we yield to the Spirit who alone can fill our hearts with God's love. But if we don't decide to stay, none of these blessings will be realized.

"It is in that stubborn staying power most preachers fail," said A. J. Gossip,[3] and he was right. But the preacher must not stand like a dumb fence post that is known only for the fact that it can stand. He must stand like the tree that sends its roots deep and its branches upward and outward, always growing, always fruitful, always helpful, in other words, the man described in Psalms 1:3 and 92:12–15.

Charles Spurgeon told his ministerial students that their motto should be, "Go forward!" Then he added, "Go *forward* in personal attainments, *forward* in gifts and in grace, *forward* in fitness for the work, and *forward* in conformity to the image of Christ."[4] He was echoing Paul's admonition to Timothy, "that your progress [pioneer advance] may be evident to all" (1 Tim. 4:15 NKJV).

The dedicated "layman" envies his pastor as a man who can devote his full time and energy to Bible study, meditation, prayer, and loving service *and get paid for doing it!* [5] Our busy members wish they could have the opportunities that we're prone to take for granted. One of the privileges of faithful ministry is that of growing in grace and spiritual knowledge and becoming more like the Master. As we enrich others, we ourselves are enriched; and the Lord is glorified.

What Phillips Brooks told his congregation applies to God's servants everywhere: "Do not pray for easy lives. Pray to be strong men and women. Do not pray for tasks equal to your powers. Pray for powers equal to your tasks."

Or, as Pastor Don put it, "It's time to grow."

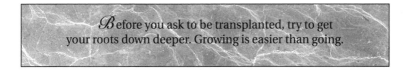

*B*efore you ask to be transplanted, try to get your roots down deeper. Growing is easier than going.

Is Our Church Maturing?

Here's a simple checklist for the pastor—not inspired or inerrant—that can help him evaluate his own ministry and the progress of the church.

1. Are the people discovering and developing their spiritual gifts?
2. Is there a place of ministry for everybody and are more people getting involved?
3. Am I working myself out of jobs or taking on more than I can handle?
4. Are we more and more going to the Bible for guidance and less and less to the church constitution, rules and regulations, and church tradition?
5. Are we all becoming more like Jesus Christ as the Spirit teaches us from the Word?
6. Is God meeting our needs in answer to prayer?
7. Am I ministering by faith, or do I "scheme" to get things done?
8. Is there a growing sense of unity and mutual concern in the fellowship? Are people spontaneously caring for each other?
9. Have we courageously scrapped some "dead ministries" and started some new ones, or are we monitoring conformity?
10. Do we have our own distinctive ministry or are we slavishly imitating other churches? Is our church a blessing to other churches?
11. Are people amazed at what's happening and does God get the glory?
12. Is the church family a witnessing community outside the walls of the church?
13. Are we sailing in unchartered waters to share the gospel with new people or aimlessly fishing in the same puddles with the same bait?

14. Do the people have a healthy appetite for the Word, and are we all happy to move into new "pastures" in Scripture? Am I riding my hobbies in my preaching?
15. Does the church have more opportunities than it has workers? Do we pray for God to raise up laborers?
16. Is the Lord calling people out of our fellowship to serve him elsewhere, and is the church family happy to send them and support them?
17. Is the Lord giving us new ideas and new challenges? Do we test them by Scripture and then courageously obey him?
18. Are the problems we face less and less personality-centered and more and more ministry-centered?

Chapter Nine

*The Power of Ministry
Is the Holy Spirit*[1]

"Don't forget Anna's recital next Friday," Marge said. "Remember, I told you that Mrs. James moved it back a week because of the basketball tournament. Anna would be brokenhearted if you missed it."

Travis hastily swallowed the last of the coffee in his cup and sat staring into space. No, he didn't remember his daughter's piano recital. Marge recognized the signal and said, "You've scheduled something else for Friday, haven't you?"

"Well, I forgot about the recital. I'm sorry, but I have more things to do than listen to kids play the piano."

"Do you have more things to do than encourage your children to use their talents to glorify God?"

Travis frowned and accepted another cup of coffee. "You're the only person I know who can turn a piano recital into a theological discussion. Of course I want to encourage Anna, but I have other responsibilities that may be more important."

"Another seminar?" asked Marge.

"Yes." Travis knew how Marge felt about seminars.

"Let's see," said Marge, "the last three seminars you attended were about understanding Generation X, building growth groups, and teaching lifestyle evangelism. What's the next one about?"

"Evangelism, church growth, and postmodernism."

"Brother!" exclaimed Marge. "With a combination like that, we ought to have revival!"

"The church could use revival," Travis said quietly, "and so could I."

Marge sat down across from her husband and took his hands in hers. "Travis, we all need revival, but I don't think another seminar is going to bring it. If the Holy Spirit doesn't give us the new life we need in the church, then it won't come any other way."

Travis was silent, thinking. "I guess it would be blasphemy to try to engineer a revival and tell the Holy Spirit what to do." He took an envelope out of his coat pocket and handed it to his wife. "This came in yesterday's mail. I don't know who sent it, but I think I know why."

The postcard Marge took out of the envelope had printed on it:

> If God were to take the Holy Spirit out of
> this world, most of what the church is doing
> would go right on and nobody would know the
> difference. [A. W. Tozer]

Both of them sat quietly for a long time, then Marge broke the silence. "Well, it's obvious that somebody in the congregation is concerned about us and the ministry of the church. They know that something is missing."

Travis said, "Marge, call Kenny and tell him I'm not going to the seminar Friday. And please manage the phone for the next couple of hours. Unless it's a real emergency, tell folks I'm not available. I'm going upstairs to have a seminar of my own with the Lord."

No matter what text he preached from, evangelist Billy Sunday kept his Bible open to Isaiah 61:1–2, the same passage Jesus used in his synagogue sermon in Nazareth (Luke 4:18–19):

The Spirit of the Lord GOD is upon me,
Because the LORD has anointed me
to bring good news to the afflicted;
He has sent me to bind up the brokenhearted,
To proclaim liberty to captives,
and freedom to prisoners;
to proclaim the favorable year of the LORD. [Isa. 61:1–2 NASB]

Some people may not have approved of Billy Sunday's enthusiastic and somewhat theatrical presentations of the gospel, but they had to admit he got the job done. At least a million people "hit the sawdust trail" under his ministry, many of them finding Christ as their Savior and Lord. What turned a baseball player into a powerful evangelist? The power of the Holy Spirit.

"The Spirit of the Lord GOD is upon me" was the secret of our Lord's ministry on earth. Though he was the very Son of God in human flesh, he labored the way he knew his followers would have to labor: in total dependence on the Spirit of God. Peter said that "God anointed Jesus of Nazareth with the Holy Spirit and with power" (Acts 10:38 NKJV), and John wrote that God gave the Spirit to Jesus without measure (John 3:34). If the sinless Son of God needed the Spirit's power for his ministry, where does that leave us, his weak and sinful followers?

About the time Billy Sunday was born, Dwight L. Moody was building his Sunday school in Chicago and keeping busy in YMCA work. After the Chicago fire, Moody went to New York City to minister at Theodore Cuyler's church. While walking down Wall Street, he had an experience with the Holy Spirit that transformed his ministry. This is how he tells it:

Well, one day, in the city of New York—oh, what a day!—I cannot describe it, I seldom refer to it; it is almost too sacred an experience to name. Paul had an experience of which he never spoke for fourteen years. I can only say that God revealed Himself to me, and I had such an experience of His love that I had to ask Him to stay His hand. I went to preaching again. The sermons were not different; I did not present any new truths, yet hundreds were converted. I would not now be placed back where I was before that blessed experience if you should give me all the world—it would be as the small dust of the balance.[2]

Like Billy Sunday, Moody was a "layman" with no special theological or ministerial training, or even ordination; yet God deigned to use him in a remarkable way. Moody would say it was the work of the Holy Spirit. "God commands us to be filled with the Spirit," said Moody, "and if we are not filled, it is because we are living beneath our privileges."[3]

When Moody ministered in Birmingham, England, in 1875, the eminent Congregational pastor and theologian R. W. Dale cooperated in the campaign. After hearing Moody preach and watching the response of the people, Dale told Moody that "the work was most plainly of God, for I could see no real relation between him and what he had done. He laughed cheerily, and said he should be very sorry if it were otherwise."[4]

In the days of the apostolic church, people were just as amazed at what God did through ordinary fishermen like Peter, Andrew, James, and John. The early church lacked many of the things that we think are essential today, like big budgets ("Silver and gold I do not have" [Acts 3:6]), college and seminary degrees ("they were uneducated and untrained men" [Acts 4:13 NKJV]), political clout ("Did we not strictly command you not to teach in this name?" [Acts 5:28 NKJV]), or even a pure church membership ("You have not lied to men but to God" [Acts 5:4 NKJV]).

What, then, was the secret of their ministry? "And they were all filled with the Holy Spirit" (Acts 2:4 NKJV). But the Spirit's fullness wasn't a luxury enjoyed only by a few pious leaders; it was the everyday experience of the entire church. "And when they had prayed, the place where they were assembled together was shaken, and they were all filled with the Holy Spirit" (Acts 4:31 NKJV).

In New Testament language, "to be filled with" means "to be controlled by." To be "full of hypocrisy" (Matt. 23:28) means to live a life controlled by playacting and pretense. "Full of anger" (Luke 4:28) means "controlled by anger," and "full of envy" (Acts 13:45) means "controlled by envy." When we are filled with the

Spirit, we are energized by the Spirit—thinking, desiring, and doing what the Spirit wills for us.

But when the Spirit's in control, the believer isn't out of control because the "fruit of the Spirit is . . . self-control" (Gal. 5:22–23) and "the spirits of the prophets are subject to the prophets" (1 Cor. 14:32 NKJV). The person who's full of wine loses control and becomes a fool, but the person filled with the Spirit gains even more control and lives wisely (Eph. 5:17–18). Any so-called spiritual experience that robs people of their God-given intelligence and self-control is not from the Holy Spirit. Perhaps some people who think they're filled with the Spirit are in actuality fooled by the spirits.

However, let's not allow the excesses and counterfeits of some people to rob us of the real blessings that the Spirit alone can confer on all who will yield to him. Either God is accomplishing his will in and through us by his Spirit, or we're doing our own thing in our own way and passing it off as the work of God. People with enough talent and charisma can often convince a church that God is at work, when all that's really happening is only orchestrated by religious "spin doctors" who don't know the difference between manipulation and ministry.

You can't franchise the blessing of God. Peter made that clear when he told Simon the sorcerer to keep his money and not try to purchase the Spirit's power (Acts 8:18–24). While there's certainly an element of the sovereignty of God when it comes to the Spirit's working (John 3:8), there's also a sense in which the Spirit responds to the heart that's thirsty for him and prepared for his coming. Jesus promised, "If anyone thirsts, let him come to Me and drink. He who believes in me, as the Scripture has said, out of his heart will flow rivers of living water" (John 7:37–38 NKJV). Then John added, "But this he spoke concerning the Spirit . . ." (John 7:39 NKJV).[5]

Almost every servant of God reaches a "longing stage" when we find ourselves searching for the "secret" of the fullness of the Spirit. If we read enough books on the subject, we find ourselves getting confused. One writer says there are "three steps" to the Spirit's fullness, while another writer, just as spiritual, claims there are "ten steps." This theologian tells you to stop searching "because you got it all when you trusted Christ," and another says just as emphatically, "There's still more land to be claimed."

We need to remind ourselves that God's blessings are determined by his soverign will. Since the wind of the Spirit blows where he wants to blow, you can't predict what he will do or control the way he will work in your life. Not everybody will have a "Wall Street" experience like Moody, nor is everybody supposed to, but any sincerely devoted servant of God can know the power of the Spirit in ministry. To quote A. W. Tozer again: "The Spirit-filled life is not a special edition of Christianity. It is part and parcel of the total plan of God for His people."

Since the Spirit of God is the *Holy* Spirit, it's plain that he isn't going to fill a dirty vessel. Unless we're deadly serious about holy living, the Spirit won't give us what we need for serving God effectively. We need the Spirit for Christian character, as well as for Christian service. To ask for God's power while ignoring God's holy standards is only to tempt the Lord and lie to the Spirit. To seek the power of the Spirit without the fruit of the Spirit is to put asunder what God has put together.

The Spirit of God is also the "Spirit of truth" (John 14:17; 15:26; 16:13), which implies that there can be no place for deception in the life of a Spirit-filled believer. Christians are to put away lies and live according to God's truth (Eph. 4:17–5:14). Whenever a lie starts to control our lives, Satan goes to work; but whenever we believe and obey God's truth, the Spirit goes to work.

But something else is implied: the Spirit of truth uses God's truth—the Word of God—when he works in our lives. The Holy Spirit gave us the Word of truth (2 Tim. 3:15–16; 2 Peter 1:20–21), and he helps us understand it (John 16:12–13) and remember it (John 14:26) so we can obey it in daily life. A comparison of Ephesians 5:18–33 and Colossians 3:16–4:1 reveals that to be filled with (controlled by) the Spirit of God means to be filled with (controlled by) the Word of God; for in both instances, the believers are joyful, thankful, and submissive to one another. It's inconceivable that we could ignore the Word of God and still enjoy the blessings of the Holy Spirit.

The Spirit was given, not to glorify himself, but to glorify Jesus Christ. "He shall glorify me," said Jesus (John 16:14). So, if our motive for service is other than the glory of Christ, we can be sure the Spirit won't assist us. The holy anointing oil given to the priests was never to be used for common purposes or duplicated for "secular" uses (Exod. 30:31–33). To do so was to invite divine discipline. We don't "use" the Holy Spirit so we can glorify ourselves; he uses us to glorify Christ.

Acts 1:8 tells us that the Spirit empowers us so we can bear witness to Jesus Christ. If my aim in ministry is other than bearing witness to Christ, then I'll have to do it without the Spirit's power. Witnessing isn't the high-powered, smooth talk of the salesperson, nor is it the clever arguments of the theological debater. Witnessing is the Spirit's revelation of Jesus Christ through the life and words of one of Christ's faithful disciples. It's the answer to the plea of the Greeks, "Sir, we would see Jesus" (John 12:21 KJV).

Often the Holy Spirit glorifies Christ in our weakness, as Paul wrote, "For when I am weak, then am I strong" (2 Cor. 12:10). Weakness that knows itself to be weakness becomes strength, but strength that knows itself to be strength only becomes weakness. Samson felt powerful when he woke up to fight the Philistines, but his strength had departed from him. David knew he was weak as he approached the Philistine giant Goliath, but God transformed that weakness into strength. Samson was interested in pleasing himself; David was concerned about glorifying the Lord.

In the brief conclusion to his exhaustive treatise on homiletics, John A. Broadus wrote: "After all our preparation, general and special, for the conduct of public worship and for preaching, our dependence for real success is on the Spirit of God."[6]

Dr. D. Martyn Lloyd-Jones concluded his valuable *Preaching and Preachers* with an entire chapter on the ministry of the Holy Spirit in the life and work of the preacher. Among other things, he said:

> We all tend to go to extremes; some rely only on their own preparation and look for nothing more; others, as I say, tend to despise preparation and trust to the unction, the anointing and the inspiration of the Spirit alone. But there must be no "either/or" here; it is always "both/and." These two things must go together.[7]

In other words, we don't tempt God by expecting the Spirit to do what we must do, nor do we grieve the Spirit by counterfeiting what only he can do. The faithful servant studies the Word, meditates, prays, gets to know the church family, and seeks to meet their needs, always depending on the Lord to give that special help that can come only from heaven. "The right way to look upon the unction of the Spirit," said Lloyd-Jones, "is to think of it as that which comes upon the preparation."[8]

But preparation is much more than sitting in the study, poring over our books. It also means praying, obeying the will of God, witnessing, loving and serving God's people, and seeking to do all to the glory of God. That's the kind of preparation the Spirit can anoint.

In his insightful lecture "The Holy Spirit in Connection with Our Ministry," which every minister ought to read and take to heart, Charles Haddon Spurgeon says: "To us, as ministers, the Holy Spirit is absolutely essential. Without Him our office is a mere name. . . . If we have not the Spirit which Jesus promised, we cannot perform the commission which Jesus gave."[9]

Our blessed Lord shall have the last word: "Apart from me you can do nothing" (John 15:5 NIV).

> We cannot organize revival, but we can set our sails to catch the wind from heaven when God chooses to blow upon His people once again.
>
> G. Campbell Morgan

Chapter Ten

The Model of Ministry Is Jesus Christ

When the applause stopped, Keith smiled at the banquet guests and said, "Thanks for such a warm response. Well, the chairman of the board told me I was supposed to say a few words, and I'm glad for the opportunity.

"First of all, I appreciate all of you coming out for this special occasion. Dr. and Mrs. Spaulding have been the shepherd and shepherdess of this flock for thirty years, and now you've asked Verna and me to take their place. We're highly honored. Of course, nobody can take their place. The Spauldings are too special for that. But we'll do our best to keep building this ministry in which they've invested so much of their lives.

"When I came here five years ago to be Dr. Spaulding's associate, I was about as green as a young preacher could be—but I don't have to tell you that! You probably remember the first time I preached here. [*Ripples of laughter*] I'm doing my best to forget it! [*Loud laughter*] But you didn't know what happened behind the scenes after that fateful Sunday morning. I have Dr. Spaulding's permission to tell you."

Keith paused and took a sip of water, heightening the suspense.

"Dr. Spaulding took me out for lunch on Monday and the conversation started with him asking me a question: 'You're a great admirer of Billy Graham, aren't you?' I admitted that I was and then asked him how he found out. He smiled and said, 'The whole church found out yesterday morning. Your voice, your style of delivery, your use of the phrase "the Bible says"—I think I counted twenty-six times you used it—well, son, it was a dead giveaway.'

"After that, I tried my best to be myself, but I kept latching on to one famous preacher after another. I guess I was insecure and thought that imitation was the best way to succeed. Anyway, I think I worked my way through Chuck Swindoll and Charles Stanley and W. A. Criswell, and Dr. Spaulding would always pin me to the wall and say, 'Son, we called Keith Fowler, not somebody else. Be yourself—that's all God wants.'

"Now, you need to know, folks, that young pastors like me need role models because that's the best way to learn. And it didn't take me long to discover that Verna and I had the best role models right here—Dr. James F. Spaulding and his wife Marian." [*Loud and prolonged applause*]

"My wife and I have watched Dr. and Mrs. Spaulding these five years, and we've learned a lot. The Fowlers and the Spauldings have worked together, prayed together, laughed and cried together, made visits together, and planned together. Now, after five years of this happy togetherness, Verna and I and the church family have to say goodbye to them as they leave us to retire near their children in California.

"But I must say one more thing before my time is up. As I began to model myself after Dr. Spaulding, a strange thing happened: I began to be more like Keith Fowler, a much improved Keith Fowler! I started discovering my own gifts and my own 'voice.' I didn't have to worry about imitating somebody else. And then I discovered why this happened: Dr. Spaulding models himself after Christ, and as I followed him, I was following our Lord. After all, Jesus Christ is the greatest role model for any pastor, young or old.

"Verna and I want to thank Dr. and Mrs. Spaulding for modeling the ministry so capably, not only to us but to the whole church family. In everything, you sought to follow the Lord. Verna and I can't be like you, nor should we even try. But we can be like Christ, who you've so faithfully served all these years.

"I want this congregation to know that, by the grace of God, your new pastor and his wife want more than anything else to serve you and the Lord just the way Jesus would if he were on earth today. That's our heart's desire, and we want you to pray daily that we'll achieve it, to the glory of God."

Our Lord never pastored a church, but he did shepherd a small group of men whom he lovingly called his "little flock" (Luke 12:32). The way he ministered to them is a good example for any of us to follow.[1] You don't have to be an apostle to be able to say with Paul, "Imitate me, just as I also imitate Christ" (1 Cor. 11:1 NKJV). All you need is a willingness to submit to Christ and follow his example as recorded in Scripture. Here's how Thomas à Kempis opens his devotional masterpiece:

> He that followeth Me, walketh not in darkness," saith the Lord. These are the words of Christ, by which we are admonished how we ought to imitate His life and manners, if we will be truly enlightened, and be delivered from all blindness of heart. Let therefore our chiefest endeavor be, to meditate upon the life of Christ. . . . But whosoever would fully and feelingly understand the words of Christ, must endeavor to conform his life wholly to the life of Christ.[2]

Nobody becomes a Christian by trying to follow Christ's example because salvation is God's gift to those who repent and believe. But nobody has the right to be called a Christian who ignores the example of Christ and doesn't seek to follow him. If ministry means anything, it means following Christ and becoming more like him as we serve others and help them become more like Christ. Becoming more like Christ is a quest that will never end in this life; but when this life ends, having been on that quest will make the next life that much more blessed.

What theologians call "sanctification" is simply the process of following Christ and being transformed by the Spirit into his likeness. We may not even know that this transformation is taking place, but others will see it and take note that we're becoming more like Jesus. And the enemy sees it and will do all he can to oppose us. The important thing is not to look into the mirror and measure our progress, but to look by faith to Christ and see how far we have to go.

More than anybody else in God's family, ministers of Christ must become more and more like Christ and fashion their ministry after his. Too often, we act like the apostles and debate over who is the greatest, instead of following the example of Christ and finding somebody to serve. If the apostles wanted to see vivid examples of the competitive quest for power and recognition, all they had to do was look around at the Roman officials and their soldiers. The Romans were masters of organizing people, exercising authority, and getting things done (Mark 10:35–45).

It's good to be organized and efficient *as long as you have the heart of a servant;* otherwise, you may end up using and abusing people instead of helping them. Remember, the nature of ministry is service; and Jesus is our model for the kind of service God accepts and blesses.

Our Lord's service on earth was the outflow of his relationship to his Father. Early in the morning, he would go off by himself and pray, seeking his Father's guidance (Mark. 1:35–39). Though he was eternal God, Jesus still had a human body with its self-imposed limitations; therefore, he had to pray, trust the Word, and depend on the power of the Spirit, even as his followers must do today. Satan tempted him to use his divine power for himself, but Jesus chose to use his power for others.

His motive for ministry was to please the Father. "I do always those things that please him" (John 8:29 KJV). Even his enemies recognized that Jesus wasn't moved by flattery or swayed by public opinion. The Pharisees and Herodians said, "Teacher, we know you are a man of integrity and that you teach the way of God in accordance with the truth. You aren't swayed by men, because you pay no attention to who they are" (Matt. 22:16 NIV). What they said was right, even if their motive for saying it was wrong.

Jesus was gentle and forgiving toward broken sinners, but stern and resolute toward people who were proud and hypocritical. He never called a repentant sinner a "child of the devil," but he did use that phrase to describe the Pharisees (John 8:44; and see Matt. 12:34). No wonder Jesus attracted sinners (Luke 15:1–2) while the Pharisees repelled them, for Jesus was a shepherd seeking the lost (Luke 15:3–7) and a physician making house calls on the spiritually sick (Luke 5:27–32). Who wouldn't respond trustfully to that kind of a friend?

The next time you're tyrannized by a demanding schedule, try to imagine what Jesus experienced day after day, as all kinds of people with all sorts of problems came for his help at all hours of the day and night. The apostles saw these needy people as nuisances and tried to get rid of them, but Jesus was moved with compassion, rebuked the Twelve, and opened his arms and heart to those who came (Matt. 14:15; 15:23; 19:13–15). His sermons were interrupted (Luke 12:13), and so were his meals and quiet retreats (Mark 6:31–33), but doing the Father's will was the nourishment of his heart. "My food is to do the will of him who sent me, and to finish his work" (John 4:34 NKJV).

It's a mystery how ministers can read and study the four Gospels, and even prepare lessons and sermons about our Lord, and still miss the glorious truth that Jesus had the heart of a servant. To "preach Christ" but not practice servanthood is to tear apart what God has put together, and God has put them together because they belong together. Jesus was a leader who served and a servant who led, and his great heart of love— for the Father and for the people—held this leadership and servanthood together and kept them balanced.

As you meditate on Jesus Christ, the model servant, you have to take into consideration what Paul wrote in Philippians 2:5–11.

> Let this mind be in you which was also in Christ Jesus, who, being in the form of God, did not consider it robbery to be equal with God, but made himself of no reputation, taking the form of a servant, and coming in the likeness of men. And being found in appearance as a man, he humbled himself and became obedient to the point of death, even the death of the cross. Therefore God also has highly exalted Him and given Him the name which is above every name, that at the name of Jesus every knee should bow, of those in heaven, and of those on earth, and of those under the earth, and that every tongue should confess that Jesus Christ is Lord, to the glory of God the Father. (NKJV)

Servanthood begins with *an attitude*, the same kind of attitude Jesus had while he was still with the Father in heaven. It wasn't a grasping attitude that said, "What's mine is mine; I'll keep it!" or "What's yours is mine; I'll take it!" Rather, he said, "What's mine is yours; I'll surrender it." In a society that too often applauds authority and achievement, no matter how it is attained, this kind of attitude may not be too popular, but it's the only attitude that God will accept and bless.

If Jesus is our model for service, then we will live for others and not for ourselves, and we will do it "for Jesus' sake" (2 Cor. 4:5). "Let each of you look out not only for his own interests, but also for the interests of others" (Phil. 2:4 NKJV). One of the remarkable paradoxes of Christian service is that we nourish ourselves as we take care of others. In bearing the burdens of others, we gain new strength to bear our own burdens; in weeping with others, our own vision is cleared and focused. Henri Nouwen is right: "The beginning and the end of all Christian leadership is to give your life for others."[3]

Of course, we can adopt the "CEO approach" to pastoral leadership, and distance ourselves from our people without ever paying the price of compassion, but that approach is very unlike Jesus Christ. Compassion is costly, but a hard heart costs even more. God help the church whose shepherd has no love for the sheep! How can spiritual leaders ever hope to minister in public if they don't have the time or the concern to minister to people's needs in private?

Preaching the Word is vitally important, but it isn't enough just to speak the truth. We must speak the truth *in love* (Eph. 4:15). Distant and unfeeling ministers ultimately discover that many parts of the Bible are closed to them because they don't have the right heart attitude to understand or expound on these texts. The Parable of the Good Samaritan is a case in point. How can ministers who spend their time "on the other side" ever hope to persuade people to imitate the Samaritan and get involved meeting the needs of others? The Good Shepherd gives his life for the sheep; the hireling finds an excuse to escape.

Jesus was crucified. It was a form of death so humiliating and painful that the cross was never discussed in polite Roman society, any more than we would discuss the gas chamber or the electric chair. Jesus changed all of that, of course, and now because of him, we can glory in the cross. But there are times when the servants of God appear to be the helpless victims of evil enemies (read Psalm 22), and that's when we discover the deeper meaning of "I am crucified with Christ" (Gal. 2:20).

Crucifixion is one form of death you can't inflict on yourself; all you can do is surrender. Like Jesus in the Garden, we *submit* to our enemies, but we *surrender* to the Father, praying, "Not my will but Thine be done." The Father is in complete control, and he is never closer to us than when we share in the fellowship of Christ's sufferings (Phil. 3:10). "We always carry around in our body the death of Jesus," wrote Paul, "so that the life of Jesus may also be revealed in our body" (2 Cor. 4:10). The grain of wheat must die if it wants to be fruitful (John 12:23–26).

Jesus prayed. Jesus depended on the Father. Jesus nourished himself in doing God's will. Jesus had compassion on people and sought to help them. Jesus sacrificed to put others ahead of himself. Jesus died for a world that didn't deserve it. This is the model God's servants need to follow, no matter how popular it may be to do otherwise.

But following the example of Jesus Christ involves much more than mere *imitation*; it involves *incarnation*. In our own strength, we can't begin to live as he lived and serve as he served. To claim that we can is tantamount to blasphemy. Ministers who feel themselves adequate for the task are only confessing how inadequate they are. Through the power of the Holy Spirit, however, we can begin to manifest the character and conduct of our Lord and share his compassion with others. "I have a great need for Christ," said Charles Spurgeon, "and I have a great Christ for my need."

Ministers need to read the four Gospels frequently and note how Jesus "pastored" different kinds of people, especially his own disciples. We must saturate ourselves with the "Christ of the Gospels" so that the Holy Spirit can reveal Christ's example to us and, when we need it, remind us of what Jesus did. We also need to saturate ourselves with the "Christ of the Epistles" and learn how the example and teachings of Jesus were applied in the early church. The "Christ of the Gospels" is indeed the "Christ of the Epistles," and there's no conflict or contradiction.

Whenever we read a book on pastoral theology or attend a ministerial seminar, we must filter everything we learn through this grid: "What would Jesus do?" The question isn't simple nor are the answers always easy, but at least this gets us started in the right direction toward the solutions to our pastoral problems. Centuries of unbiblical religious music, art, and tradition can rob us of the true Christ and the way he pastored people. There's no substitute for peeling off the stereotyped ideas that blind us and allowing the Spirit to show us the true Christ.[4]

One thing stands out clearly: Jesus accepted people as they were and adapted his approach to meet their needs. He never manipulated people toward his "standard procedure" because he had no "standard procedure." There was no room in his ministry for religious "sales talks" or memorized cookie cutter conversations. He found the metaphor that best fit the sinner's need and went from there. To the woman at the well, he spoke of living water. With Nicodemus, he discussed the new birth. To the critical Pharisees, he spoke of lost sheep and concerned physicians. Each pastoral encounter was new and adventurous because he was led by the Spirit and loved people too much to manipulate them.[5]

Nor was our Lord always "successful" with every person who sought him. The rich young ruler went away sorrowful, nine lepers never thanked him for healing them, and Judas went out and hanged himself. Some of the people who saw him raise Lazarus from the dead turned state's evidence and went to his enemies and reported what he did. After preaching a powerful sermon on "the bread of life," Jesus watched his crowd evaporate. Jesus wept over Jerusalem because the people were ignorant of what God wanted to do for them. Humanly speaking, there were seeming failures, but from the divine perspective, all that he did pleased the Father and accomplished his will. It was the people who failed, not the Lord.

However, we frail humans have our times of failure, and sometimes these defeats hurt us deeply. At board meetings, we see some of our best ideas ground into the carpet. In pastoral calling, we exit from homes or hospital rooms with something less than the peace of God left behind. At the close of counseling sessions, we feel drained and defeated because apparently nothing was accomplished. How do we handle these experiences and still follow the example of Jesus?

Our Lord always expressed his emotions honestly. He grieved over the scribes' hardening hearts (Mark 3:5) and sobbed over Jerusalem's unbelief (Luke 19:41). He wept quietly at the grave of Lazarus (John 11:35), and expressed displeasure when his own disciples criticized Mary of Bethany (John 12:1–8). He responded to unbelief by saying, "O faithless and perverse generation, how long shall I be with you and bear with you?" (Luke 9:41 NKJV).

It does no good to disguise a broken heart or a discouraged spirit just to give the impression that we're "victorious." At the same time, it does even more harm to major on our wounds in painful isolation instead of coming to the Great Physician for healing. When we're feeling defeated, we have to admit it honestly, accept it humbly, leave it with the Lord believingly, *and go on with our work devotedly*. "We must leave to God all that depends on Him" wrote Fenelon, "and think only of being faithful in all that depends upon ourselves."

It does us good to share our feelings, fights, and failures with a "true yokefellow" (Phil. 4:3) who can listen patiently, see clearly, and respond genuinely. Painful as it may be occasionally, accountability has a way of keeping us moving toward maturity and not just looking for sympathy. "As iron sharpens iron, so a man sharpens the countenance of his friend" (Prov. 27:17 NKJV). "A recluse is always a very one-sided man," wrote H. A. Ironside.[6] We were made for society; God never expected us to bear our burdens alone.

God has a way of turning defeats into victories, not to save our pride, but to glorify his name. Measured by human standards, the Jesus we seek to imitate was a failure. In spite of this, at the close of his earthly ministry, Jesus was able to say to his Father, "I have glorified you on the earth. I have finished the work which you have given me to do" (John 17:4 NKJV).

That's what we want to imitate most of all.

> *P*aul "travailed in birth" that Christ might be formed in his people (Gal. 4:19). Ought we not to travail that Christ might be formed in us?

Conclusion

Two Open Letters

Dear Roger:

Thanks for your phone call and letter, although I'm sorry to hear about the situation in the church. However, don't be discouraged! It's never too late to get a new strategy for keeping the flock together so that all of you can joyfully serve the Lord. I went through it eight years ago, you'll recall; so let me share my own experience.

The first clue I had that something was starting to go wrong was the news over the grapevine that some of our younger families were "church hopping." This really upset me and I too quickly decided—the old male ego!—that they were backsliding and ready for a pastoral visit. But before I had a chance to call on them, they called on me. According to my notes, the conversation went something like this:

Greg: Pastor, we don't want to hurt you, but we feel there's something missing here in First Church. Several of the younger couples have talked about it and prayed about it, and we've been visiting other churches to see what they're doing.

Me: Well, there's always room for improvement. What are you looking for?

Duane: That's the whole trouble—we don't know!

Me: Then how will you know when you find it?

Greg: Pastor, we know it sounds crazy, but when we find it, we'll know it. Something down inside will tell us.

Me: Isn't that a bit dangerous? I mean, you wouldn't take that approach if you were choosing a physician or a dentist. [*This "logical approach" didn't get to the root of the problem. I was too defensive. I needed to listen.*]

Duane: Pastor, we haven't abandoned the Bible or prayer. If anything, we've been reading the Bible more and praying more than ever. But we have some unhappy campers in the young couples' fellowship and we hate to see that happen.

Me: Well, let's do this: let's all get together some evening over coffee and pie and talk about it. I'm willing to listen and learn, and I promise you I'll share what I learn with the elders. We'll do what we can to make First Church a place where you and your children can worship the Lord and serve him happily.

Duane: Pastor, please understand that we're not trying to run the church. We know there are other people here who may have different ideas, and we don't want to cause trouble.

Me: Duane, you never cause trouble when you speak the truth in love and sincerely try to make the church more effective in ministering the Word. Now, let's select a date.

Well, we met and talked and prayed, and then we met again. Gradually the Lord showed me that I really wasn't in step with the younger members of the church. When you've been in a church for over twenty years, it's easy to get comfortable and stop growing, and that's what had happened to me. As you know, Roger, the elders decided to add a younger associate pastor to the staff, a man who could one day become senior pastor. He and I worked together to build a program that would attract and hold the younger crowd without alienating the older generation. It wasn't easy, and more than once Pastor Mark and I had to do a lot of praying and yielding. By the blessing of God, however, it worked! You know the rest of the story.

So, my counsel to you is:

1. Accept the "unhappy campers" and humbly listen to them. If their hearts are right, they'll help you better understand yourself and the church. "Love never fails."
2. Admit to areas in your own life that need "tuning up." The younger folks need to catch up with the past, but you and I need to catch up on the present. Be honest.
3. Keep your church leaders informed and involved, and never allow any "generation bashing" from either side. We belong to each other and we need each other.
4. Get everybody praying! Give yourself time to discern the will of the Lord. Don't be pressured, but don't be so slow in responding that people give up.
5. Once you know what God wants you to do, do it, no matter how many people threaten to leave or how many prophets predict gloom and doom. We can't please everybody, nor should we try; but Romans 12:18 is still in the Bible.

The church that monitors conformity and never changes will quietly die, but the church that changes too fast will quickly commit suicide. Blessed are the balanced! It's the behind-the-scenes, prayer-saturated pastoral ministry, with both the old and the young, that will get the job done. Believe me, I know!

We're praying for you and the church. Keep us posted.

Your friend,
Warren

Dear Herb:

Thanks for meeting with me yesterday to let me unload my concerns about "the state of the church." Talking to a "veteran" servant like you really helps, as does listening to the wisdom you've gleaned over the years. Your sense of humor lightened the load, as did your willingness to be vulnerable. It's encouraging to know that other pastors have had their embarrassing and difficult times.

It occurred to me as I drove home that the people in your congregation are older than the people I serve. I read somewhere (how's that for precise documentation?) that the pastor's age tends to be the median age for the congregation, which may explain why things that work for us don't work for you.

We both know that music is a land mine. The folks over sixty want only the classic hymns; and if we use choruses, we have to go back to the fifties to get them. But the generation younger than I am wants "contemporary Christian music" with a beat that encourages clapping and endless repetition. Our worship leader and I try to blend and balance both styles in our services. I'm sure neither group is completely satisfied, but we're convinced that generations need to learn from each other.

One thing you said especially provoked my thinking: "If older believers are unhappy with today's generation, who do they think trained them?" In the church you pastor, most of the leaders grew up in the church family and never knew what it was like to be "outsiders." But when I look at our congregation, I realize that most of our leaders are first-generation believers! They didn't all have the benefits of growing up in a church that taught the Scripture and gave them models of spirituality to follow. The complaint you often hear from your people is, "It's not the way it used to be!" When somebody says that to me at our church, I take it as a compliment! We're all growing together.

Thanks for pointing out Psalm 78:3–4 and reminding me that each generation has to "pass the torch of faith." But our families are so busy that it's difficult to get them to commit themselves to the traditional schedule of Christian education opportunities. However, we're finding that the "growth group" approach is working well, and God is giving us a new generation of leaders who are very serious about discipleship. But whatever changes we make in our program or methods, we agree with you that the Word of God must be central in everything.

Whenever I've worshiped at your church, I've always appreciated the congregation's sense of reverence in the sanctuary; and I can sense that you get nervous if there's noise or any distractions. In our church, the congregation acts more like spectators arriving at a gymnasium for a basketball game; and I'm doing my best to educate them to show more reverence. However, if there is a lack of reverence, it's mainly because of the "entertainment" mentality that dominates today's culture, and not because our people don't honor God. My generation grew up with television and is visually oriented to "sound bytes," while your generation grew up with radio and learned how to listen, be quiet, and use their imagination.

Yes, the dress code for church has changed. From the time I could walk to Sunday School, I wore a coat and tie; but my son isn't following my example (and this keeps Sunday mornings peaceful). I guess I'm unwilling to see style of dress (within reason) as a theological statement. I would rather have our students come in jeans and T-shirts than not come at all; and as for women wearing slacks to church, well, that seems to be the norm these days. "Man looks at the outward appearance, but the Lord looks at the heart" (1 Sam. 16:7 NIV).

In summarizing our conversation, Herb, you taught me that the dynamic of ministry is really change; but there are some things that must not change. As pastors, we must be both change agents and conservationists; and that's not an easy job. What I need more and more is discernment. "Test all things; hold fast what is good" (1 Thess. 5:21 NKJV).

I appreciate your flexibility about change. Some older pastors I know just complain about how the churches are different from what they used to be, and they dream about "the good old days." You aren't like that. In fact, you're the one who told me ("the young guy") that I have a responsibility not to gripe. Thank you!

Herb, you are a good mentor, and I thank you for letting me learn from you and even "see into" you. May God's grace and peace fill your life and ministry!

Your friend,
Dave

Chapter 1: The Foundation of Ministry Is Character

1. It must be admitted that the professions try to maintain high standards and exercise discipline when necessary. The church may not always be as diligent as the professions in handling these matters, but we're trying to do better.

2. Batsell Barrett Baxter, *The Heart of the Yale Lectures* (Grand Rapids: Baker Book House, 1971), 30–31.

3. Phillips Brooks, *Lectures on Preaching* (Grand Rapids: Baker Book House, repr. 1969), 9. Brooks was addressing the all-male classes of the Yale Divinity School and so used the words "man" and "men" frequently. We today would interpret the words generically as meaning mankind, humans in general. His famous definition of preaching as "the communication of truth through personality" would demand that Brooks emphasize personality (character); otherwise, the message can't get through as it should.

4. Phillips Brooks, *Sermons* (London: Richard D. Dickinson, 1879), 66.

5. Andrew A. Bonar, *Memoirs and Remains of Robert Murray M'Cheyne* (London: Banner of Truth Trust, 1966), 282.

6. See *The Integrity Crisis* by Warren W. Wiersbe (Nashville: Oliver/Nelson, 1988).

7. Ralph G. Turnbull, *A Minister's Obstacles* (New York: Fleming H. Revell, 1946), 23. Baker Book House reprinted a revised edition of this classic in 1972, and in 1979 published the companion volume, *A Minister's Opportunities*. Both books ought to be in every pastor's personal library and frequently read.

8. Galations 6:1 teaches that it's possible to be tripped up suddenly and fall into sin; but even then, the sinners have nobody to blame but themselves. Granted, one sudden transgression may not be as heinous as many habitual sins; but the sinner still has to take the responsibility. A life of deliberate, habitual sin is an indication that the person has never been born of God (1 John 3:4–10). We never lose the ability to sin, but we can conquer the appetite for sin.

9. Good and godly people in the church disagree as to whether a minister who has been immoral should be allowed to pastor a church again, even if there has been successful restoration; and we must not make our convictions a test of fellowship or spirituality. Some saints make a distinction between ministers who suddenly fall and commit an act of immorality (Gal. 6:1) and those who develop a pattern of repeated sin. Since more is involved than the personal spiritual restoration

of the offender, each situation must be considered individually. Has the person lost so much stature that it would be difficult to exercise authority in a church? Would a place of ministry become a place of temptation? Would the restored servant be better off working under authority than in a leadership role? In the exercise of Christian discipline, there's no place for shallow sentiment that masquerades as Christian love. True repentance is costly and real forgiveness is not cheap. "But there is forgiveness with you, that you may be feared" (Ps. 130:4 NKJV). However, we want to avoid extreme positions that assume authority not given to us by the Scriptures. David expressed this fear perfectly when he said, "Please let me fall into the hand of the LORD, for his mercies are very great; but do not let me fall into the hand of man" (1 Chron. 21:13). In exercising discipline, we must see to it that mercy and truth meet together so that righteousness and peace can kiss each other (Ps. 85:10).

Chapter 2: The Nature of Ministry Is Service

1. For a discussion of what ministry is and what it means to be a servant-leader, see *On Being A Servant of God* by Warren W. Wiersbe (Nashville: Oliver/Nelson Publishers, 1993).

2. Quoted in Thomas C. Oden, *Classical Pastoral Care,* vol. 1 (Grand Rapids: Baker Book House, 1994), 12. The quotation is from *To The Shepherd* by John Climacus.

3. John R. W. Stott, *The Preacher's Portrait* (Grand Rapids: Eerdmans, 1961), 101.

4. Dr. and Mrs. Howard Taylor, *The Biography of James Hudson Taylor* (London: China Inland Mission, 1965), 316.

5. Ibid., 245.

6. John Wesley, *The Works of John Wesley,* vol. 2 (Grand Rapids: Zondervan, n.d.), 420.

7. Peter's admonition that we "desire the pure milk of the word" doesn't contradict either 1 Corinthians 3:1–3 or Hebrews 5:12–14. His emphasis is on desire and not diet. He urges us never to lose our appetite for God's truth, even in its simplest form. Just as a healthy baby has an almost insatiable appetite, so God's children must crave the Word of God.

8. William Purcell, *Onward Christian Soldier* (London: Longmans, Green and Co., 1957), 2.

9. Wayne A. Meeks, *The First Urban Christians* (New Haven: Yale University Press, 1983), 11.

10. In ancient days, the word "shepherd" was applied to anyone in official leadership, including kings, princes, and priests. However, we don't violate Scripture if we apply these words to the pastors of local churches.

11. Every large church is really a collection of smaller churches. If the sheep aren't organized into "care groups" that are shepherded by spiritual leaders, the pastors will gradually get out of touch with the needs of the people and not be able to minister to them. Christians belong to each other and need each other, so they ought to see it as a privilege to serve each other.

Chapter 3: The Motive of Ministry Is Love

1. William Jewett Tucker, *The Making and Unmaking of the Preacher* (Boston: Houghton Mifflin, 1898), 163.

2. John Newton, *Voice of the Heart* (Chicago: Moody Press, 1950), 288.

3. Charles H. Spurgeon, *Metropolitan Tabernacle Pulpit*, vol. 24, 249.

4. Ibid.

5. Warren W. Wiersbe, *On Being a Servant of God* (Nashville: Thomas Nelson, 1993), 3.

6. The title "shepherd" applied primarily to the political leaders of that day, especially the kings and officials. However, in the nation of Israel, the corrupt priests and the false prophets were just as guilty of abusing God's sheep. "An astonishing and horrible thing has been committed in the land: the prophets prophesy falsely, and the priests rule by their own power, and My people love to have it so. But what will you do in the end?" (Jer. 5:30–31 NKJV).

7. Phillips Brooks, *The Influence of Jesus* (London: H. R. Allenson, n.d.), 191.

Chapter 4: The Measure of Ministry Is Sacrifice

1. John Henry Jowett, *The Preacher: His Life and Work* (New York: Harper and Brothers, 1912), 114. This is one of the best volumes in the "Yale Lectures on Preaching" series.

2. Henri J. M. Nouwen, *The Wounded Healer* (Garden City, N.Y.: Doubleday and Company, 1979), xv–xvi.

3. James Boswell, *The Life of Samuel Johnson*, vol. 2 (London: J. M. Dent, "Everyman's Library" edition, 1973), 218.

4. G. Campbell Morgan, *The Westminster Pulpit*, vol. 8 (London: Pickering and Inglis), 283.

5. The Greek word translated "perfect" in this verse also means "to mend nets" and is so translated in Mark 1:19.

Chapter 5: The Authority of Ministry Is Submission

1. See 3 John 9–11 and Acts 20:30.

2. Some recent secular management books are beginning to catch the idea that a successful manager must manifest integrity and have the heart and mind of a servant, but they don't identify integrity and service as "Christian virtues." They are only means to the end of "getting things done" in the company.

3. See *Humility: The Beauty of Holiness* by Andrew Murray (New York: Fleming H. Revell), a little devotional gem that deserves much more attention than it gets.

Chapter 6: The Purpose of Ministry Is the Glory of God

1. Quoted in Ralph Turnbull, *A Minister's Obstacles* (New York: Fleming H. Revell, 1946), 45.

2. Bramwell Booth, *Echoes and Memories* (New York: George H. Doran Company, 1925), 34.

3. Brooks, op. cit., 106–107.

Chapter 7: The Tools of Ministry Are the Word of God and Prayer

1. This is illustrated symbolically in Exodus 17:8–16, when Israel fought the Amalekites. Moses on the mountain, his hands lifted to heaven, pictures inter-

cessory prayer; and Joshua fighting in the valley pictures the power of the Word, "the sword of the Spirit" (Eph. 6:17; Heb. 4:12). It took both for Israel to gain the victory.

2. Charles Haddon Spurgeon, *Lectures to My Students* (London: Marshall, Morgan, and Scott, 1965), 43.

3. Just because some advocates of "spiritual warfare" have departed from Scripture and turned to their own extravagant ideas doesn't mean we should abandon this vitally important part of the Christian life. After all, Ephesians 6 was written to believers! See *Released from Bondage* by Neil T. Anderson (Here's Life Publishers, 1991); *Winning the Invisible War* by E. M. Bounds (Whitaker House, 1984); *Kingdoms At War,* by Bill Bright and Ron Jenson (Here's Life Publishers, 1986); *Overcoming the Adversary,* by Mark Bubeck (Moody Press, 1984); *I Believe in Satan's Downfall,* by Michael Green (Eerdmans, 1981); *Spiritual Warfare,* by Timothy Warner (Crossway, 1991); and *The Strategy of Satan,* by Warren Wiersbe (Tyndale, 1979).

4. There are twelve instances of prayer in the Book of Nehemiah: 1:5–10; 2:4; 4:4, 9; 5:19; 6:9, 14; 9:5–37; 13:14, 22, 29, 31.

5. G. F. Barbour, *The Life of Alexander Whyte, D.D.* (London: Hodder and Stoughton, 1923), 297.

Chapter 8: The Privilege of Ministry Is Growth

1. See 2 Corinthians 2:16 and 3:5–6.

2. Thomas Merton, *New Seeds of Contemplation* (New York: New Directions Books, 1961), 194–95.

3. Arthur John Gossip, *In Christ's Stead* (London: Hodder and Stoughton, 1925), 114. A recent survey indicates that the average pastor is forty-six years old and has been in ministry eighteen years. But average pastoral tenure has shortened from seven years per church to just under five years. Ten percent of those surveyed have made no moves, twenty percent have moved five to seven times, and ten percent have moved eight times or more. Sixty percent have moved two to four times. Only eighteen percent changed churches because of unresolved conflicts or tensions in the church (*Your Church,* May/June 1995 [vol. 41, no. 3], 56.)

4. Charles H Spurgeon, *Lectures To My Students* (London: Marshall, Morgan and Scott; 1965), 205.

5. This is not to minimize the special burdens and problems that come with faithful ministerial service, but every vocation has its own "occupational hazards." The pastor would do well to realize that the people in the church don't have easy lives simply because they aren't in full-time ministry! They have their battles and burdens just as he does, and he would do well to sympathize with them. More than one pastor has been rudely awakened to this fact by spending a day on the job with each man on the church board.

Chapter 9: The Power of Ministry Is the Holy Spirit

1. Books about the person and work of the Holy Spirit abound. A. W. Tozer's *The Divine Conquest* is a classic (Revell, 1950), as is John R. W. Stott's *The Baptism and Fullness of the Holy Spirit* (InterVarsity Press, 1964). See also: *Keep in Step with the*

Spirit by J. I. Packer (Revell, 1984); *The Divine Comforter* by J. Dwight Pentecost (Revell, 1963); *The Spirit of God*, by G. Campbell Morgan (Revell, 1953; Baker repr., 1981); *The Person and Work of the Holy Spirit*, by Rene Pache (Moody Press, 1954); *The Mystery of the Holy Spirit* by R. C. Sproul (Tyndale, 1990); and *The Spirit of Christ*, by Andrew Murray (Christian Literature Crusade, 1964).

2. William R. Moody, *The Life of Dwight L. Moody* (New York: Fleming H. Revell, 1900), 49. For an excellent discussion of Moody's views on the Holy Spirit, see chapter 7 of Stanley N. Gundry's *Love Them In: The Proclamation Theology of D. L. Moody* (Chicago: Moody Press, 1976).

3. Quoted in *Lessons from the Life of Moody*, by George Sweeting and Donald Sweeting (Chicago: Moody Press, 1989), 91.

4. A. W. W. Dale, *The Life of R. W. Dale of Birmingham* (London: Hodder and Stoughton, 1902), 318.

5. Inasmuch as this declaration was made at the Jewish Feast of Tabernacles, when the Jews remembered their wilderness experiences, Jesus was probably referring to the water that came from the rock. The phrase "his heart" may refer to Messiah, typified by the rock, rather than to the believer. Jesus supplies the Spirit, but he had to suffer and die in order to do it. The water flows from him, not from us.

6. John A. Broadus, *On The Preparation and Delivery of Sermons* (New York: A. C. Armstrong, 1897), 504.

7. D. Martyn Lloyd-Jones, *Preaching and Preachers* (London: Hodder and Stoughton, 1971), 305. One need not agree with Dr. Lloyd-Jones' views of the baptism and fullness of the Spirit to benefit from what he emphasizes in this chapter.

8. Ibid., 304.

9. Charles H. Spurgeon, *Lectures to My Students* (London: Marshall, Morgan and Scott, 1965), 186–87.

Chapter 10: The Model of Ministry Is Jesus Christ

1. The classic work on the subject is *The Training of the Twelve* by A. B. Bruce; but see also *The Walk, Character, and Conversation of Jesus Christ Our Lord* by Alexander Whyte (Grand Rapids: Baker Book House, 1975); *The Mind of the Master* by Ian MacLaren [John Watson] (New York: George H. Doran, 1896); *The Jesus Model* by David L. McKenna (Waco: Word Books, 1977); *Master Discipleship*, by Don Hawkins (Grand Rapids: Kregel, 1996); and *Imago Christi: The Example of Jesus Christ* by James Stalker (New York: A. C. Armstrong, 1890). *Teaching as Jesus Taught* by Roy B. Zuck contains a great deal of helpful information on how Jesus dealt with crowds, "seekers," his opponents, questioners, and his own disciples (Grand Rapids: Baker Book House, 1995).

2. Thomas à Kempis, *Of The Imitation of Christ* (London: Oxford University Press, 1949), 1. This is "The World's Classics" edition. One of the best modern translations of this classic is by William C. Creasy and is published by Ave Maria Press, Notre Dame, Indiana (1989). *Of The Imitation of Christ* is a book every minister ought to read through regularly.

3. Henri J. M. Nouwen, *The Wounded Healer* (Garden City, N.Y.: Doubleday "Image Book," 1979), 72. You don't have to adopt all of the author's theology to find this book challenging and instructive.

4. See Philip Yancey's excellent book *The Jesus I Never Knew* (Grand Rapids: Zon-

dervan, 1995).

5. In *The Great Physician* (New York: Fleming H. Revell, 1937), G. Campbell Morgan presents studies of the biblical records of our Lord meeting the needs of nearly fifty different persons.

6. H. A. Ironside, *Notes On Proverbs* (Neptune, N.J.: Loizeaux Brothers, 1975), 388.

Subject Index

Scripture Index

Scripture Index

Warren W. Wiersbe is Distinguished Professor of Preaching at Grand Rapids Baptist Seminary and has pastored churches in Indiana, Kentucky, and Illinois (Chicago's historic Moody Memorial). He is the author of over one hundred books and now focuses his energies on writing, teaching, and conference ministry.

David W. Wiersbe is a pastor in the Evangelical Free Church of America. In addition to pastoring a church in Roscoe, Illinois, he has served as a chaplain of fire and rescue units and works with local support groups for the grieving. Among his books is *Gone but Not Lost: Grieving the Death of a Child.*